ANCIENT & MODERN

ANCIENT & MODERN

Peter Jones

Duckworth

Second impression July 1999
First published in June 1999 by
Gerald Duckworth & Co. Ltd.
61 Frith Street, London W1V 5TA
Tel: 0171 434 4242
Fax: 0171 434 4420
Email: enquiries@duckworth-publishers.co.uk

ISBN 0 7156 2890 9

Typeset by Derek Doyle & Associates, Mold
Printed in Great Britain by
Redwood Books Ltd, Trowbridge

Contents

Preface

In September 1991, Trevor Grove of *The Sunday Telegraph* invited me to contribute a weekly 'Ancient & Modern' column to the paper. In March 1996, at the invitation of Frank Johnson, the column moved to *The Spectator*.

The purpose of the column is to take a contemporary event and, in a few hundred words, describe for the general reader how some ancient Greeks and Romans, to judge from the surviving literature, might have reacted to it. I here arrange by topics and stitch together into a continuous narrative a selection of the four hundred columns produced so far (with thanks to *The Spectator* for release from their copyright).

Since news fades fast, the specific contemporary event to which any column originally referred has often been converted into a universal human dilemma; but the generalisations, repetition of basic information and prejudices obligatory in a popular column have not been entirely removed. There is no pretence at offering a complete account of the ancient world, let alone a balanced one.

It is a pleasure to acknowledge Andrew Morley's artwork throughout. My thanks also to the ancient Greeks and Romans for all their help. They are responsible only for their own views; they are absolved from holding mine.

January 1999   Peter Jones

Reading List

It is far better to read what Greeks and Romans say at first hand than what is written about them. My *Learn Latin* (Duckworth 1997), *Learn Ancient Greek* (Duckworth 1998) and *Classics in Translation* (Duckworth 1998) introduce the general reader to the languages and best modern translations. Of authors not covered in *Classics in Translation*, Aristotle, the two Plinys and Plutarch are never far from my elbow.

When translating I usually consulted Penguin Classics or Loeb editions. The main exception is R. Waterfield, *Plato: Republic* in World's Classics.

Of secondary sources, I found myself constantly turning to:

J.P.V.D. Balsdon, *Life and Leisure in Ancient Rome* (London 1969).
J. Barnes, *Aristotle* (Oxford 1982).
L. Casson, *Travel in the Ancient World* (second edition, 1994).
K.J. Dover, *Greek Popular Morality* (Blackwell 1974).
E. Fantham *et al.* (eds), *Women in the Classical World* (New York/ Oxford 1994).
S. Hornblower and A.J.S. Spawforth (eds), *The Oxford Classical Dictionary* (third edition, Oxford 1996).
Joint Association of Classical Teachers, *The World of Athens* (Cambridge 1984).
P. Jones and K. Sidwell (eds), *The World of Rome* (Cambridge 1997).
G.E.R. Lloyd, *Magic, Reason and Experience* (Cambridge 1979).
J.T. Roberts, *Athens on Trial* (Princeton 1994).
O.F. Robinson, *The Criminal Law of Ancient Rome* (Duckworth 1995).

Notes

Capital letters in a sub-heading indicate the introduction of a new topic. There is a Time chart on pp. 169–73 and the maps are on pp. 174–7

Eros with his bow and arrows

1

Sex and Marriage, Life and Death

STOP, IN THE NAME OF LURVE

Wonderful thing, lurve. These days it is defined by pop-stars impregnating series of girl-friends, breaking up, professing 'disillusion', and vanishing to 'think things through'. For Greeks and Romans, this would have made a splendid subject for comedy (see p. 141). Otherwise, ancient lurve did not bring children into the equation – they were far too important to be associated with such frivolous activities. 'Sex' or 'lust', *eros*, was the main interest. But were children not the inevitable consequence? That all depended on who you were having the sex with.

Passions like lust were seen in the ancient world as irresistible external forces, imposing themselves from the outside. One could therefore have no control over them (the excuse is still popular). *Eros* in particular was seen as a kind of madness – a heaven-sent *mania*, both irrational, because one so often fell in love with the most unlikely people, and inexplicable, because it attacked with such speed. The poetic image of a malicious little boy, armed with arrows and spraying them around at random, is an effective one for this most baffling phenomenon. So when one had been subjected to the assaults of Aphrodite (or Eros, Latin Cupid, with his bow and arrows) there was little one could do about it. If the object of one's desire responded, all well and good. If not, one moped one's life away – till the next assault.

Whatever the outcome of Aphrodite's attack, the result (for poets at any rate) was withdrawal from the world – the gratified lover because he needed nothing other than his love, the ungratified because life could not be lived without his love. But at some stage one usually stated that one had grown up and it was time to consider another life style. Here the Greek poet Philodemus (*c.* 110-35 BC) goes into the routine:

I fell in love. Who hasn't? I partied. What's new? I had been driven mad. By whom? By Aphrodite. To hell with her. My hair is getting grey now, announcing I am at the age of discretion.

When it was time to play, I played. That's over. Now wiser counsels will prevail.

'Stars' say something equally hackneyed when their hair starts greying
too.

Woe, men

The problem with taking the 'helpless victim of *eros*' approach was that
it made one appear weak-willed. 'No man is free who is not master of
himself' said Epictetus (AD 55-135), a stern saying in the modern world
where inventing new needs, failing to satisfy them and then moaning
about the resulting 'insecurity' and 'sense of failure' enslave people
daily. The ancients valued their freedom and independence above
everything else, and felt that dependency (let alone on pointless
'needs') was the enemy of freedom. So even working for someone else
was looked down on because it made you dependent upon someone
else for your existence (see p. 103). But it was especially degrading to
be in thrall to one's sexual urges which, on top of everything else,
laid one open to a risk no Greek would ever willingly incur – being
laughed at.

It was therefore important for those who did fall into the honey-
trap – especially if they were old and grey – to have ready-made
excuses. The ineffable treachery of women was the one Greek males
usually came up with. The seventh-century BC poet Semonides wrote a
poem comparing women to different animals, all but the bee being
unfavourable. So the sow-woman lived in permanent squalor; the
bitch-woman always yapped about nothing; while the mare, 'fastid-
ious, avoids all housework, milling, sieving and cleaning in case she gets
dirty. She bathes and perfumes herself three times a day, always
combing and decking her hair with flowers, lovely for someone else to
look at, but unless one is an MP or Chief-of-Staff [the original says
'tyrant or king'] who can afford to indulge himself like this, she is
nothing but trouble.' All the woman's fault, in other words – though
when the MP in question was David Mellor, it is hard to think of
another rational explanation.

Epicurean philosophers like the great Roman poet Lucretius (*c*. 100-
55 BC) took an especially tough stance on this. If one was to live true to
the teachings of the Greek philosopher Epicurus (341-271 BC), one had
to live free of pain, and lustful passion was one of the greatest pains of
all. It was, says Lucretius, like a 'festering sore', growing with nourish-

ment, and turning men into idiots. It made men 'behave as though blinded by love, and credit the beloved with charms to which she has no valid claim'. So, Lucretius goes on, a sallow wench becomes a 'nut-brown maiden', and a dishevelled slut is commended for her 'sweet disorder'. If her eyes are green, they become 'green as Athene's'; if she is thin and gawky, she is 'lithe as a gazelle'. Midgets become 'sprites, a delight from top to toe', giantesses 'daughters of the gods, divinely tall'. Does she have a speech defect? No, 'a charming lisp'. Is she speechless? No, 'wonderfully modest'. Bad tempered? She 'burns with a gem-like flame'. Half-dead with coughing, she is 'delicate'; vast-bosomed, 'Ceres suckling Venus'; fat-lipped, 'all kiss'; skinny, 'svelte and wil-lowy'. Venus *could* be enjoyed, insisted Lucretius, but only by the healthy, not the love-sick. Seeing the truth about the beloved was the key to healthy understanding. He would not have approved of St Valentine's Day.

Cynical philosophy

Another way out of the trap was a hard-bitten cynicism. In his dia-logue *Phaedrus*, the Greek philosopher Plato (*c.* 429 - 347 BC) puts such an account of *eros* into the mouth of the orator Lysias. Lysias argues that people newly in *eros* are not to be trusted because their judgement is warped, and they are incapable of seeing what is in their best inter-ests. So they are hurt if the beloved drops some innocent remark. They suspect the worst if the beloved has any other friends. They overlook any sign of stupidity in the beloved, they boast wildly of any kind of success, and when their first passion dies, nothing is left. Recriminations follow, and the lover regrets the benefits he has bestowed and the little he has got back for his attentions.

So, Lysias argues, it is far better not to fall in *eros*. The man not affected by this madness will suffer none of these defects. He will coolly calculate the advantages the relationship can bring. He will not be hurt by remarks not meant to harm; he will encourage other friend-ships; he will not be blind to the beloved's weakness; he will not embarrassingly broadcast his *eros* to all and sundry; and since there is no 'first passion', there is none to die. Who needs passion? Fathers and sons don't. So he will 'share his possessions with his beloved when he grows old and remain firm friends when looks have vanished'.

Cynical - or realistic? A little cold calculation never comes amiss when one is dealing with something as hot-to-handle as *eros*. Plato, however, did not think of *eros* as a self-interested desire for something in the beloved that will benefit you (in those terms, how could a father love his son?). He commandeered the term for his own philosophical purposes. Far from being about the acquisition of benefits, he thought, *eros* was all to do with the nature of the lover. Essentially, for Plato, it was a form of desire for philosophical truth, the manifestation of a search for higher knowledge, leading from mere earthly beauty to the ultimate Good. Not a chat-up line your average 'star' employs.

Having it both ways

Plato and Lysias were, of course, talking about homosexual *eros*. That, for aristocratic Greek males, was a higher form of *eros* than heterosexual, perhaps because it was directed at someone who was your equal, not a dependent inferior (as they tended to see women). No one who engaged in such relationships was regarded as effeminate or queer. Nor did they preclude Greek males from being married and fathering children too. Upper-class Greeks were bisexual: homosexual relationships were not a substitute for heterosexual relations but an agreeable addition to them.

Unlike us, Greeks did not inherit a set of divinely ordained beliefs prescribing correct sexual behaviour. Custom was king, and the form that Greek homosexuality took was pederasty – not boys but adolescents (most desirable when the first down appeared on their cheeks). The historian Herodotus (fifth century BC) boasted that the Persians picked up the idea from the Greeks. When the comic poet Aristophanes in his *Birds* (414 BC) dreams of a Utopia, where one is free of all usual social restraints (see p. 83), he imagines a world in which a father with a good-looking young son would come up to you, deeply hurt, and say 'What's all this I hear about you and my boy? You meet him coming from the gymnasium, freshly bathed – and what do you do? You don't kiss him, you don't talk to him, you don't cuddle up to him, you don't tickle his balls – and you an old family friend!'

This passage hints at the usual double standards so common in sexual matters – in unAristophanic real life, a father would be shocked at his son receiving treatment he would happily give any attractive young male. But the theory was that a young man would be flattered to receive the attentions of a wealthy, influential, adult male, and could be educationally improved by him (by imitating the older male's example) in ways that would benefit the community (see p. 130). But it was not 'done' for the adolescent to show enthusiasm for such sexual relationships, let alone to be penetrated. That would be to allow himself to be treated like a woman, not at all the ticket for a brave young Athenian (male prostitution was left to non-Athenians, and enthusiasm for male advances was confined to women). From the evidence of Greek pottery, fondling the young boy's testicles, followed perhaps by inter-crural intercourse, may have been as much as the male could hope for.

When the adolescent grew a beard, he was no longer desirable to males. In the normal course of events he would now turn his attention to girls – and sooner or later, young adolescents too. In other words, for all the prevalence of pederasty among the upper classes, there does not seem to have been what we would call a 'gay' culture in ancient Athens. Indeed, any male who professed a desire for adult males was regarded as a rather odd fish (see p. 130).

Kinky, by Jove

Greeks were as fascinated by sexual behaviour as we are, and Greek myth is full of bizarre goings-on undreamed of in even the most imaginative politician's philosophy. For copulation purposes Zeus turned himself into a swan with Leda; a shower of gold with Danae; and a bull with Europa. When his wife Hera became suspicious of his activities, he would turn his lovers into animals to hide them, e.g. Callisto into a bear and Io into a cow.

The mythical male prophet Teiresias even underwent a double sex-change, into a female and back into a male again. Zeus then enquired of him who got more pleasure out of sexual intercourse, the male or female, and Teiresias replied the female, by a 9-1 ratio. Hera at once blinded him for giving away woman's great secret. One can speculate endlessly about what that myth might mean. Since women (evidently) got nine times more pleasure than men during love-making, the myth certainly validated Greeks' belief that women must be sex-mad and therefore (perhaps) to be carefully watched over, especially in male company.

Kinkiest of them all, and proving to Greeks just how far women would go, was surely Pasiphae, wife of King Minos of Crete. When Minos failed to sacrifice a particularly handsome bull to the sea-god Poseidon, the god punished him by making Pasiphae fall in *eros* with the animal. Desperate to consummate the affair, she persuaded the inventor Daedalus to construct a framework looking like a cow into the rear of which she could insert herself. The deed was done, and the product of this union was the Minotaur ('Minos-bull'), a bull-headed man that Minos promptly had shut up in the labyrinth. All this is the very stuff of House of Commons' parties.

In his *Symposium*, a round-the-table dialogue on the nature of *eros*, the Greek philosopher Plato puts an amusing account of the origins of humanity, with a bizarre sexual twist to it, into the mouth of one of the participants, the comedian Aristophanes. (We do not know whether this get-together has any historical reality, but the tale Plato gives Aristophanes is certainly very Aristophanic.) Originally, says Aristophanes, there were three sexes – male, female and hermaphrodite. But they were not like us physically. Each was a double-person with one brain but two faces, four arms and four legs, and so on, like two ordinary humans joined back to back. Being very powerful, they decided to attack the gods.

Zeus, not wishing to destroy creatures who sacrificed to him, decided to weaken them fatally instead. So he told Apollo to slice them in half, turning the face and neck to the cut side. Apollo obeyed, slicing, smoothing and reshaping the new bodies like a top plastic surgeon, drawing the skin together over the belly like a purse with strings (whence the navel) and providently moving the genitals to the front as well. So, concluded Aristophanes, each of us is really half of a whole, and our sexual orientation is homosexual if we were originally all male or all female, and heterosexual if originally hermaphrodite. We spend our lives, then, seeking our other half, and if we find them, there is no greater joy. We want to be with them for ever, and if we could, we would like to be physically rejoined with them. This is true *eros*, lasting for ever, far more than just a temporary passion.

But, as we have seen, whatever Plato meant by giving Aristophanes this wonderful speech, he wanted *eros* to have a purpose beyond physical gratification.

Marriage-go-round

Where does what we call 'love' come into all this? The Roman poet Catullus (first century BC) is the first to talk of relationships in terms of an intense, idealised lasting bond or treaty, though with someone not his wife, as if marriage did not come in the same category. In the ancient world, marriage was first and foremost about having legitimate children, which preserved the family line and conferred on the children the right to inherit both their father's status and property (see p. 13). The fourth-century BC Greek orator Demosthenes (addressing, as ever, an audience of citizen males) puts the whole issue succinctly when he says 'We have courtesans for pleasure, concubines for our day-to-day bodily needs, and wives to bear us legitimate children and to be loyal

Seeking our other half

guardians of our households'. That utterance does not mean that such patterns of behaviour were compulsory or necessary. Love in our sense does not seem to have been touted as a necessary ingredient of marriage, but that is no reason for arguing that it was not.

What women made of all this is impossible to tell. Ancient literature is largely composed by wealthy males with strong political connections, and they are going to give a version of events creditable to themselves and adjusted for public, predominantly male, consumption because that is the predominant audience for ancient literature. All one can do is try to understand the social and moral categories that males deployed.

Aristophanes in his comedy *Lysistrata*, for example, shows the women of Athens staging a sex-strike to persuade their husbands to end a war and restore family life. This would make little sense if wives found no sexual satisfaction in marriage or if husbands routinely found theirs outside it. The Roman politician-philosopher Cicero (first century BC) in his letters writes warmly and lovingly of his wife Terentia. He was writing for posterity and publication: he clearly felt it was creditable to express these feelings. Inscriptions on tombstones often express sentiments about married love that we would recognise. *traicit et fati litora magnus amor*, says the Roman poet Propertius (first century BC) in a poem that imagines a dead wife addressing her husband: 'great love crosses even the shores of fate'. But if sex, love and marriage were not so confused in the modern mind, it would at least focus attention more firmly on what marriage is *for* – the production of children, with all the ramifications that has: primarily, the best interests of the children, not the gratification of those producing them (see p. 67).

HOUSE(WO)MEN

Early feminists ordered women to come out of their households. More recent feminists, seeing the household as a 'power-base', instruct them to return. Either way, ancient Greeks would have been appalled.

The household – family, slaves, buildings, land – represented the total resources of most Greeks. It was far too important to entrust to a woman until she had demonstrated her competence. In his treatise on household management (*Oikonomika* = *oikos* 'household' + *nomos* 'law, regulation', whence our 'economy'), the soldier and essayist Xenophon (fourth century BC) explains how it should be done, in a discussion between Socrates and the wealthy Ischomachus.

Ischomachus shows how he trained his wife, an ignorant fifteen-year-old but, he says, a woman with control over her appetites (a vital consideration in a choice of wife). He taught her to stay inside and supervise the slaves (including *their* training), paying particular attention to duties involving cloth-making, grain-storage, keeping accounts and maintaining health. He showed her how to keep everything in the right place – food, wine, valuables, boots, cloaks, blankets, pots, pans, furniture – and train a slave to produce them on command. She was the guardian of the household: the ultimate responsibility for everything in it was hers. His wife, Ischomachus says, was thrilled at the prospect: tending to sick slaves especially appealed.

Even so, she still got things wrong. One day Ischomachus noticed she had put on some make-up. A stern lecture ensued: the way to look her best was healthy exercise supervising the slaves at the loom and in the bakery and storeroom. 'By Hera,' Socrates concludes, 'your wife has a truly masculine way of looking at things.' Whatever conclusions we want to draw from *that* observation, a woman's economic power was real: like Odysseus' wife Penelope who was an expert worker at the loom, married women were a major source of household wealth.

Hysterical cures

Since women's primary function in the ancient world was to produce children, ancient doctors (all male) developed a huge literature on conceiving and bearing them. They also tended to associate women's illnesses with sexual or child-bearing dysfunction – whence 'hysteria' (see p. 57). For all we *know*, women may have thoroughly agreed with them. Or they may not. We cannot tell.

The word derives from *hustera* ('womb'). Greek doctors (who did not themselves use the term *husteria*) believed that an unused womb dried up, lost weight, and began to seek moister parts of the body. It would therefore 'wander off' and relocate itself near the heart, brain, liver, rectum etc., and cause terrible trouble, both physical (shortage of breath, palpitations, gnashing of teeth) and mental (delusions, madness, suicidal tendencies).

In the light of doctors' analysis, it is not surprising that the symptoms were most commonly seen in virgins and widows, and that the most usual suggested remedy was marriage, intercourse and children. If that diagnosis could not be applied, other treatment was available. This was aimed at cajoling the womb back into place. Patients were invited to sniff horrible-smelling substances to repel the womb back to where it belonged, or sweet-smelling substances were introduced into the other end to lure it back.

Given Greek theories of how the body worked, this had a crazy logic to it (see p. 52). Perhaps prolapse of the womb suggested the womb's capacity to 'wander'. But at least Greeks treated the problem as a medical, not a psychological one. So in ancient Greece, women behaving oddly would not have been thrust into asylums and handed over to counsellors and the Freud squad, with all the attendant guilt and shame, but given aromatherapy and told to make love all day.

Womb with a view

The modern feminist trumpet gives an uncertain sound – *quot feminae, tot sententiae*. Today's harassment theory ('all men are rapists') yields to tomorrow's empowerment theory ('we are better than men'). But women had no institutionalised public voice of any sort in the ancient world. That is not to say they had no power or influence over public affairs. The fifth-century Greek politician Pericles' mistress/wife Aspasia and wives of Roman emperors like Livia (wife of Augustus) and Agrippina (wife of Claudius) were highly influential figures. In a case involving the status of married women, an ancient orator points out to the (male) jury how outraged their womenfolk will be if the jurors report home that they have voted 'wrongly'. The point is that female influence was not formally institutionalised. None of this, however, prevented ancient (male) writers making comedy, for a male audience, out of imagining what would happen if women *did* have institutional power.

In his comedy *Ecclesiazusae* ('Women in Power', 392 BC), Aristophanes envisages a world in which women control the democratic Assembly (*ecclêsia*) of Athens. They pass laws which assign all property to the community (so with no private property to fight over, there will be no law-suits) and then legislate that any man may have intercourse with any woman, and children will regard all men as their fathers. The catch is that the interests of old and ugly women will be protected by legislation which gives them the right to first go with any male.

There then follows a famous scene in which the young lover, sighing for his mistress as ardently as she for him, is accosted by an old hag who demands first turn with the young man. The girl manages, briefly, to save him from that fate, but then a second, older and uglier, hag arrives who drives off the young girl and herself claims the man. But not for long: enter a third, still older and uglier, hag who attacks the second hag and claims priority for herself. The scene ends with the young man being forced into the second hag's house, with the third hanging on like grim death.

Aristophanes famously played the same male fantasy game of women-power with *Lysistrata* (411 BC), in which the wives of Athens seize the Acropolis (where the money was kept) and stage a sex-strike to force their men to stop the war and restore family life. But if Plato saw these comedies, he may have been set thinking by them. At any rate, his provocative proposals for his ideal state give roles to women that would have left most Greeks opened-mouthed in astonishment, Aristophanes probably most of all. Unless Aristophanes got the idea from Plato ...

Female guardians

In his *Republic*, Plato argues (through his constant mouthpiece, Socrates) that a ruling class, the Guardians, should control the ideal state (see pp. 101, 124). They would act like the guard-dogs of a flock. But female guard-dogs hunt and protect just like the males (though the males are stronger). So, by analogy, if the state education programme produces male Guardians, it should produce female Guardians too, since the same education should have the same results.

But then comes an objection. Are not some people innately suited to some kinds of jobs? And are not females innately different from males? Possibly, says Socrates. But if the only difference turns out to be that females bear offspring and males mount females, that has no bearing on their suitability as Guardians. The question is: is there any evidence that for some professions or occupations there are *innate* differences between men and women?

None at all, Socrates argues, and for a devastatingly incorrect reason. Since men are vastly superior to women in *everything*, he concludes that there can be 'no job which belongs to men *qua* men or women *qua* women. Innate qualities have been distributed equally between the two sexes, and women can join in every occupation just as much a men, even though they are weaker in all respects.' People may be inclined differently, he agrees, but inclination has nothing to do with innate ability. Conclusion: 'women and men have the same natural ability for being Guardians of a community'. It is simply a matter of education. All very liberated.

Or not. Plato is not satisfied with simply welcoming women into the top jobs, and to explain his position describes the contemporary Athenian way of handling the 'woman' problem: 'we concentrate our resources, as the expression has it, under one roof, and let our women take charge of the stores and the spinning and wool-working in general' (cf. Ischomachus above). The consequence of this, he goes on, is to leave women under the power of their menfolk, but otherwise unregulated. But will not anyone who legislates for a mere half of the human race – the male half – get things badly wrong? The lawmaker must legislate for men and women alike, without distinction. Plato acknowledges that women will not like this: 'they have got used to a life of obscurity and retirement, and any attempt to force them into the open will provoke tremendous resistance'. But that is tough: 'we must not regulate just the men and let the women live as they like and wallow in expensive luxury'. (Again, one remembers Ischomachus' satisfaction at marrying a woman who could control her appetites.) Off, then, to the training ground and common mess-halls with the women too.

Plato's views about women, then, are not especially 'liberated' – or only to the extent that in his ideal state women will share the same slavery as men. Interestingly, the Athenian model of resource management becomes more and more appropriate to our day and age. Since modern technology makes the need for a work-place less and less necessary in certain ranges of jobs, women's liberation from male-dominated work patterns will inevitably increase. So too will men's.

WELL ENDOWED

There is no secret about the destructive effects that breakdown of marriage can have upon women with children – impoverished, jobless, they can all too easily doom themselves to a life of dependency on the state.

Greeks and Romans made a priority of a woman's security in marriage. The dowry was their answer. In classical Greece, the dowry that went with the wife remained her property in the event of divorce. The same was broadly true among Romans too, and in the sixth century AD the emperor Justinian turned the provision of a dowry from a moral into a legal obligation. The Greek historian Herodotus particularly admired the way Babylonians (Iraqis) handled the problem of providing a dowry for the very poor and marrying them off.

Every year, the villagers gathered all the girls of marriageable age into one place and offered them for sale as wives, while the men stood round in a circle. An auctioneer then started offering the girls for sale, beginning with the best-looking ones, and the rich bid against each other for the privilege of marrying them. The money so gained was put on one side. When, however, a girl attracted no bids at all, the auctioneer used the money he had taken for the beauties to re-offer the girl, together with a dowry. The man who accepted her with the smallest dowry won the bid. 'In this way,' Herodotus goes on, 'the beauties provide dowries for their ugly or misshapen sisters.'

But there were controls. The most important was that 'no one could take home a girl he had bought without finding a backer to guarantee his intention of marrying her'. The second was that, in cases of disagreement between husband and wife, 'the law allowed the return of the purchase money' and, presumably, the dissolution of the marriage.

Herodotus was full of admiration for the system. From his point of view it was liberal (all women are married off), humane (there are cast-iron guarantees and get-out clauses) and fully cash-backed. Nowadays, he laments, the system has fallen into disuse, and all girls of the lower class are forced into prostitution to relieve their poverty.

Birthrights

Family and children, not 'meaningful relationships', were at the heart of ancient society, and this is why Herodotus so admires the Babylonian system. Neither Greeks nor Romans would have many qualms about the principle of the fertility treatments that we agonise over. Healthy, legitimate children were an absolute priority for them, and they had no belief either in the sanctity of life (they exposed weak children regularly) or in gods to whom these issues were of importance. Greek myth, for example, abounds in alternative births. When Zeus impregnated Metis, he was afraid she would produce a child stronger than him – so he swallowed her. When he developed a splitting headache, the blacksmith god Hephaestus hit him over the head with an axe and out popped Athene. The god Dionysus was born from Zeus's thigh, into which Zeus had inserted him when he rescued him from his dead mother's womb. In a tragedy by Euripides (fifth century BC), the youthful woman-hater Hippolytus expresses the wish that women had no part in childbirth at all – much better just to pay a god and pick a child up off the temple floor. No problems in principle with fertility treatments, then, or test-tube babies.

But one of the purposes of children was to ensure that the family property stayed in the right hands. This may be why a newly married woman could be regarded with some suspicion by her new family: she was a dangerous alien from another family who needed to be schooled in the new family's ways before she could be trusted. Faced, then, with fertility treatments, the ancients would have been worried only if donors *outside* the family were involved. On the other hand, since the ancients attached great importance to good family breeding, it would have been a bonus if a clinic could provide semen or eggs of divine origin.

Genetic engineering would also have been welcomed by the ancients because it allowed one to choose the sex of one's children. The Spartans in particular would have jumped for joy – foolishly.

In the seventh century BC, Sparta annexed the territory of neighbouring Messenia and reduced the population to slaves ('helots'). Since the Spartans now found themselves outnumbered 5-1 by the helot population, they turned themselves into a military state. The immediate result of this was that they put all their resources into rearing male children, to be placed in army barracks at the age of seven. So there was restricted access to marriage; pederasty was common; and more females than usual may have been abandoned at birth. On top of that, Spartan inheritance laws split everything equally between all children. So (over time) they reduced their estates to virtually nothing and consequently were downgraded to non-citizen status. Small families more and more became the order of the day.

The results were disastrous. By *c.* 500 BC, bachelors were being ordered to marry to keep the birth-rate up, and if they failed, denounced in public by being forced to walk naked around the marketplace in winter, while singing that they were being rightly punished. By the fourth century BC, in a country that could support 1,500 cavalrymen and 30,000 soldiers (the fourth-century BC Greek philosopher Aristotle tells us), male citizens of military age were down to under 1,000. Desperate measures in the other direction were now taken. Wives of child-bearing age with old husbands were encouraged to take young lovers, and incentives were offered to have large families. So genetic engineering is all very well, but it has serious consequences if the social structure cannot bend to accommodate it.

Male shots

Though abortion was probably common, and contraception practised (Aristotle recommends olive-oil, which Marie Stopes found to be 100% effective, though interestingly ancient sources never mention *coitus interruptus*), ancients knew that neither conception nor childbirth could be guaranteed. Doctors and philosophers were therefore full of advice on the subject. Aristotle recommended that a woman start bearing children at 18, as wife to a man aged 37, for the charming reason that they would thus reach the end of their reproductive lives together. Prior to intercourse, women should stick to dry foods, or fast; men should eat 'strong' food and drink a little wine, while remaining sober. The semen must be hot on delivery, so Aristotle did not recommend males with long penises that would cool the semen on its travels (size *does* matter). Women must retain the seed in the womb by crossing their legs after intercourse.

Since male children were regarded as more desirable than female, there was much advice about how to beget a boy. Male semen must be dense and compact, not fluid. The man must eat plenty of hot, strong food. He should lie on his right during intercourse and tie up his left testicle. A woman could check for the sex of the child by mixing her milk with flour and baking a cake. If solid, a boy; crumbly, a girl. All this drivel is the logical consequence of Greek beliefs about health depending on a balance of the four 'humours', and particular beliefs about males being dry and hot, females moist and cool (see p. 52).

So now you have your child. But what on earth do you do with it? For us, having a child seems to be a female 'right', based on a mother's need for 'fulfilment' – in other words, the satisfaction of maternal needs (see p. 132). The ancients would not have understood this – or rather, ancient male authors do not consider it. For them, children were nothing to do with rights or fulfilment or maternal instincts. They were everything to do with specific, long-term, private, public and religious duty. First, children maintained the family line, and its fortunes, traditions, achievements, links with ancestors and worship of gods. The end of a line was a social and religious disaster. Second, children served the state by providing the necessary manpower to defend it, the main condition of survival in the ancient world. What an insult to the goddess Athene for a woman not to produce children to protect her city of Athens!

In *Lysistrata*, Aristophanes' famous comedy about the women staging a sex-strike to end the war, bring the men back, and restore family life (411 BC), the heroine Lysistrata has a moving exchange with a male official which makes many of these points:

Magistrate: You've done nothing for the war effort!
Lysistrata: Curse you, we've only taken its weight twice over –
    bearing sons and sending them out as soldiers –
Magistrate: Stop, don't open old wounds.
Lysistrata: Then, when we ought to be enjoying ourselves in the

prime of life, we sleep alone because of the campaigns. No more about us, though – but I grieve for the young girls growing old in their beds.

Magistrate: Don't men grow old?

Lysistrata: It's not the same. When a man comes home, however grey he may be, he can soon find a girl to marry. But a woman's chance slips quickly by and if she doesn't take it, no one wants to marry her, and she's left sitting at home, grasping at any omen that looks hopeful.

There is no romance here. This is ruthless, hard-eyed, unflinching pragmatism. In the ancient world, marriage and children are what women are for, in their interests as much as in men's and the state's.

Adopt-a-bloke

It is therefore extremely interesting that adoption was so popular in the ancient world. What on earth were families doing giving away their precious little ones? But they were not little. Adoption was far too serious a business for babies to be involved.

Adoption was largely an upper-class institution, and in the power of the father, not the mother, to transact. Its purpose was not to care for the unwanted, let alone to satisfy emotional needs, but to ensure that the family inheritance was passed on to the most favourable person (sometimes at the expense of legitimate sons) in order that it survive and flourish. Greeks even used to get sons adopted in order to escape family debts (one of the few tricks the fraudulent millionaire newspaper-owner Robert Maxwell missed).

For an aristocrat in this position, adoption was rather like marriage. He would survey the market of spare sons among his aristocratic and successful friends and relations, and hope to make a deal with the best available prospect, who would then pass fully into his family. Hence, no babies: only adults need apply. It was big business. From AD 14-200, for example, only three Roman emperors were survived by natural sons. It was mayhem out there, as families tried to get their sons taken onto the imperial gravy train. Agrippina, for example, married to the emperor Claudius, wheeled and dealed endlessly to get Nero, her son by her previous marriage, adopted. She finally got her way, and when Claudius died in 54 BC, Nero succeeded to the imperial throne. But Nero promptly had Claudius' natural son Britannicus murdered, just to be on the safe side.

There is a lot to be said for Roman-style adoption. Perhaps it would solve all the problems of the monarchy.

GOOD FOOD GUIDE

Doctors often praise Greek diet, which has remained in many ways the same since classical times – all that olive oil, lots of veg., and not much meat, let alone sugar (a rarity in 1650, ubiquitous by 1850). Not that ancients knew it was healthy. Life-expectancy was too low for diet alone to kill them, and for most people, there was nothing else to eat except what was on offer from their land. Only the rich few could eat the much-vaunted (and cholesterol-filled) 'pig that had died from over-eating'. Chefs, however, were treated with the same contempt as artists (see p. 133). Ancient Greeks would have been appalled at the way we grovel before these self-important technicians, fighting to gain tables at their restaurants as if we were serving them, rather than they us.

When the Greek comic poet Teleclides (fifth century BC) envisaged a golden age, he wrote 'Every torrent ran with wine; barley pastes fought with wheat loaves to reach men's lips first; fish came to the house, baked themselves, and served themselves up at table; rivers of soup, swirling with meat chunks, flowed by couches; honey cakes sprinkled with spices sat on dishes; and thrushes, served with milk cakes, flew down men's gullets.'

Hardly luxury, but day by day a Greek peasant would see little change from barley-based pastes, gruels and flatbreads, olives, figs, goat's cheese and water. If the Homeric epics were full of meat-eating, that was food for heroes. The only time the average Greek would taste meat would be at a communal sacrifice. Oxen were far too valuable as bulk-transporters to eat.

But meat was not such a luxury as fish, which Greeks loved to soak in good, strong sauces – bitter herbs, cheese and onions, sometimes balanced with honey and olives, rather like our port and stilton. They also had a taste for *liquamen*, a liquid drained off from barrels of rotten salted fish. Spartan diet was the worst. Of their 'black broth' (pork-stock, vinegar and salt), a visitor commented 'No wonder they are so brave: anyone else would die a thousand deaths rather than have to face it'.

Good drink guide

Wine played an important part in ancient diet, and experiments to beef it up were common. So ancients would not have understood the modern penchant for fining wine-makers thousands of pounds for adding synthetic flavouring, regarding such additions as jolly sensible. In his *Natural History*, the Roman encyclopaedist Pliny the elder (AD 23-79) goes into the detail of the additions made to ancient wines. Rough African wines, for example, were softened with gypsum or lime, while in Greece a wine's softness was enhanced with potter's earth, marble-dust, salt or sea-water (best taken from the deep sea during the spring equinox, evidently).

Best of all was the Italian (not primarily Greek) habit of mixing resin with the pressed grapes to add scent and piquancy, and Pliny describes the taste of various resins from Arabia (sharp), Palestine (strong), Syria (like honey) and Cyprus (the best of them all). He recommends plenty of resin for strong, fiery wines, less for thinner, flatter ones, and goes on to say that sulphur, and the ashes from vines and oakwood, could also be used. Colouring was added, and wine could be boiled in lead casks to sweeten it (not recommended).

Pliny was lost in admiration at the human ingenuity that went into producing wine from anything going – fruit (figs), herbs (hellebore), vegetables (turnip) and shrubs (juniper), etc. So he would have thought our wine-laws daft. As one remembers those stupendous Burgundies of yore consisting largely of Algerian red wine, condensed milk and horses' hooves, one has to agree.

Outside festival celebrations, serious drinking among the upper classes was especially prevalent at the male symposium ('drink-in') or dinner-party, where women, boys and song were also freely available. The wine (up to *c.* 18% alcohol content) was diluted (one part wine to two or three water) in a large mixing-bowl, which was constantly refilled. The going could get tough. The wise man was recommended to leave after three mixing bowls: 'the fourth leads to violence, the fifth to uproar, the sixth to revel, the seventh to black eyes, the eighth to summonses, the ninth to vomiting and the tenth to madness and throwing things about.' But we do not hear of alcoholism – perhaps because drinks were always diluted.

At the end of the Greek philosopher Plato's philosophical dialogue *Symposium* on the nature of love, there is a wonderful picture of the discussion being broken off by the irruption of a crowd of drunken revellers and everyone really getting stuck into the alcohol. Gradually people disappear or collapse, till finally only Socrates is left, arguing that a writer of tragedy should also be able to write comedy. Socrates, naturally, is immune to the effects of drink. As dawn breaks the last two symposiasts drop off. Socrates makes them comfortable and leaves, spending the day 'as he normally did'. Wonderful thing, philosophy.

Party policy

We all become lost for words at dinner parties. Help is at hand. In the fifteen surviving books of his *Deipnosophistai* ('The Gastronomers'), the Greek dinner-party expert Athenaeus (*c.* AD 200) goes into every sort of detail of the conduct of parties, right down to a well-ordered checklist of suitable topics of conversation. The talk concentrates on four main areas: food, drink, music and sex. Everything there is to be known about cooks and cooking – Greek, Persian, Sicilian, Roman, and others – is extensively discussed. Food is submitted to intensive analysis for its various properties, healthy and otherwise, and elaborate and strange banquets from all over the known world described. Kitchen equipment is considered (there is a fine passage where a world is imagined in which the food cooks and serves itself, and then the dishes wash themselves up). Moral issues arising from eating – gluttony and abstention, luxury and frugality – are bandied about.

Drink and music are subjected to the same scrutiny as is sex (there is a thought-provoking story about Spartan women thrashing their men into affection for them). More important than anything, however, all discussion is supported by literary examples. Some 1,250 authors, the titles of a 1,000 plays, and 10,000 lines of verse are cited – a literary gold mine, since many of these verses survive nowhere else.

It is not surprising, then, that the Greek poet Simonides (556-468 BC) said wine and literature were discovered at the same time. The tragedian Aeschylus (525-456 BC) used such extraordinary language that people assumed he composed in a vinous frenzy. 'Drink water and you'll never produce a work of art', said the Greek comedian Cratinus (fifth century BC). The Roman poet Horace (68-5 BC) said poets smelled awful at night because they never stopped drinking by day.

School drinks

Today's world is full of busybodies expressing their opinions about 'the drink problem', of course, none more so than the Portman Group with its various 'voluntary codes of practice'. It is a pity that Plato is not one of this sinister group. He would tell them to abandon the whole idea.

Plato's admittedly somewhat reluctant theory on the benefits of under-age drinking is expounded in his last work, *The Laws*, in which he lays down the practical rules which should guide life in his ideal republic. It is in the context of his educational agenda that he cautiously welcomes alcohol into the debate.

Plato argues that, used in moderation, drink has two important effects. First, it releases the inhibitions and shows people in their true light. This gives the educators invaluable insights into the real character of the young people they are trying to educate. Second, it beneficially reorganises and reshapes the drinker's 'soul'. This makes the young more malleable and thus more susceptible to sound advice, and the old (who do the teaching) less grumpy and censorious and so more agreeable to the young. In particular, the young can be rendered mildly plastered under controlled conditions, when their equally plastered elders can educate them in that self-discipline and resistance to pleasure so vital for a happy Platonic existence. The theory is that if they can resist temptation drunk, they can resist it under any circumstances.

Drink, in other words, is a great educational benefactor. Plato's advice would be to get it off the streets, where it really is dangerous, and back where it belongs – in the classroom.

GOING MAD ON HOLIDAY

Tired but happy we return from holidays, ready for a well-earned rest. But if the 'father of history', Herodotus, is anything to go by, our holidays may have revealed us in our true light – raving mad.

Herodotus is following the career of the Persian king Cambyses (d. 522 BC). After attacking Egypt, Cambyses began to behave increasingly oddly. He broke open ancient tombs, jeered at gods' statues, and even burned them, 'assaulting and making mockery of everything which ancient law and custom have made sacred in Egypt'.

Herodotus draws a weighty conclusion from this behaviour: Cambyses was nuts. His reasoning goes as follows. 'If anyone, no matter who, were given the opportunity from choosing amongst all the nations of the world the beliefs which he thought best, he would inevitably, after careful consideration of their relative merits, choose those of his own country'. Herodotus explains why: 'everyone without exception believes his own native customs and the religion he was brought up in to be the best' and illustrates the proposition with a telling example.

When Darius was king of Persia (522-486 BC), he invited Greeks who happened to be at his court to say what they would take to eat the dead bodies of their forefathers. Appalled, they said they would not do it for any money in the world. Later, in the presence of the same Greeks, he asked some Indians (who did in fact eat their parents' dead bodies) what they would take to burn them. 'They uttered a cry of horror and forbade him to mention such a dreadful thing.'

Custom, Herodotus concludes, is 'king of all' – and therefore Cambyses was off his rocker. Only a card-carrying, five-star lunatic would go about mocking what law and custom had made sacred to other peoples. Oh dear. As we return from foreign parts, can any of us maintain that we were innocent of casting aspersions upon local practices?

Rocky horror

One of the main problems of holidays around ancient ruins is that we are never quite certain what it is we are seeing. Trotting around the Greek sites clutching our *Blue Guides*, we may idly wonder how they *know* what this heap of stones or that monument actually is. Step forward the Greek travel writer, Pausanias.

Between AD 160-180, Pausanias composed his ten-book *Description of Greece*. He is not much interested in views, local produce or wildlife (though he does mention the honey of Hymettus and a singing trout in Arcadia). What excites him are the sacred places and monuments of Greece, especially the temples and sanctuaries, and the history, myths and legends associated with them. So it is places like Olympia and Delphi, massively rich in such monuments and all still surviving at the time, that receive the best coverage. Pausanias' system for handling this project is to divide Greece into areas, and begin by outlining an area's history. Then he takes the quickest route from its boundaries to the main city, describing anything of interest on the way, and makes for the city centre. After describing the centre, he describes the streets that lead into it. Then he journeys from the centre along the main roads that radiate out of the city to other important places in the region (and back), again describing everything of importance *en route*. The whole area covered, he hops over the boundary into the next area, and starts again.

Pausanias did not invent the guidebook (we read of examples from the fourth century BC), but his alone survives. Without him, much of Greece and the details of many sites (especially ones like Olympia and Delphi) would be unidentifiable. Traveller, salute him.

Swanning about

Many tourists these days travel round the Mediterranean by sea. We should thank Poseidon we sail in a modern ship. A high-ranking Roman official would travel in a flotilla of oar-driven galleys. This was very slow, but at least he would dock every night, eat in a restaurant and sleep well. Most sea travel, however, took place between April and October in sail-driven cargo ships (max. 6 knots). The prevailing Etesian winds, blowing from the north, made journeys from e.g. Rome to Egypt a matter of a fortnight; but since the ships did not tack effectively, the return could take up to two months, via the South Turkish coast, Crete and Sicily.

The passenger (and cruise) ship is in fact a nineteenth-century invention. Till then, travellers went to the docks, asked around for a ship going in their direction, and then waited for however long it took for winds and omens to come good. St Paul, travelling from Palestine to Rome, caught first a boat to South Turkey (Myra), and then picked up a grain-ship on its long haul back to Rome from Egypt. Such vessels could be massive, the biggest holding over a thousand tons of grain, not to be matched again in Europe till the seventeenth century.

A VIP on a large Roman boat, which could hold up to 600 passengers, might get a small cabin, but nothing more. Passengers took their own bedding, pots and pans for cooking, slaves to wait on them, and enough food and wine to see them through to the next port. They would sleep at night on the open deck, putting up an awning if they had one. Cooking would be shared with the crew in the ship's galley. Instead of the 'captain's table', important people were given a chair on the poop to chat with him. In a storm, everyone was set to work (St Paul helped jettison the tackle and then the grain cargo). The alternative was death. There were no lifeboats.

Nowadays, there is a fashion for truly vast ships holding thousands of passengers. But for all their gigantic theatres, swimming pools, health spas, etc., none can compare for sheer class with the *Syracusia* (240 BC). Designed by Archimedes for Hiero II, tyrant of Syracuse, it had interior panelling of cypress, ivory and aromatic cedar. Multi-coloured mosaics telling the story of the *Iliad* covered the three floor-levels. Statues and art-work were liberally scattered about, and there was a temple to Aphrodite, the ship's guardian deity, paved with agate. The promenades were decorated with arbours of white ivy, plant beds and vineyards, all providing shade and regularly watered.

It contained a gymnasium and a bath with three copper tubs and a fifty-gallon basin. It had twenty stables, a sealed water-tank in the bows (20,000 gallons), and a sealed fish-tank, packed with fish. The captain's cabin, sensibly located next to the kitchens, was of 'fifteen-bed' size, with three 'three-bed' size rooms off. It was so vast it needed Archimedes to invent the screw-windlass to launch it. *And it was not even a cruise ship.* It was a cargo boat, protected by fearsome armaments (Archimedes again), carrying 400 tons of grain, and 500 tons each of pickled fish, wool and other cargo.

But Hiero hit problems. It was too big for most harbours. What to do? Knowing his friend Ptolemy of Egypt had a large harbour and a grain shortage, Hiero promptly renamed it *Alexandris*, filled it with grain and *gave* it to him. Now *that* is class.

Shopping customs

Whatever else we do on holiday, however, shopping for souvenirs is always a priority. It has ever been thus. A glass bowl has been unearthed in Afghanistan, decorated with a picture of the harbour in ancient Egyptian Alexandria. The souvenir business was alive and well in the ancient world too.

The bay of Naples was Rome's favourite holiday resort, and there the Roman souvenir-hunter could buy little glass vials with labelled pictures of the major sights in the area: 'Lighthouse', 'Nero's Pool', 'Oyster Beds', etc. When St Paul went to Ephesus *c.* AD 52, he famously ran into trouble with Demetrius the silver-smith, who sensed a threat to his trade in miniature replicas of the famous temple of Artemis (Latin Diana) there. Serious antique-hunters went to Rome, the centre of the art trade. The poet Martial (first century AD) satirises one Mamurra, who spends all day in the antique market, checking out tables, chairs, couches inlaid with tortoiseshell ('too small'), the number of emeralds and size of pearls in the jewellery, and winds up buying a pot for 10p.

But customs charges still had to be faced, due at all ports, frontiers and provincial boundaries in the Roman Empire. The traveller presented a list of everything he had with him. Only conveyances and objects 'for personal use' were exempt: even corpses being transported for burial were charged. Dues were low (2%-5% of value), but luxury items like silks, perfumes, spices and pearls ran to 25%. Undeclared objects were confiscated; newly bought slaves disguised as family-members were released on the spot; and lawyers debated whether customs officials could actually touch married women who stowed pearls away in their bosom. As today's officials rifle through our bags, we may feel, like Plutarch (second century AD), 'irritated and upset that they go through bags not their own, searching for hidden items – yet the law allows it'.

Sightseeing

Finding your way around in ancient cities was not easy. Sightseeing, as now, was always a strain. Most Greek and Roman cities did not have street signs or house numbers. Since side-streets were unlit, one toured cautiously by night; and by day, as one travel writer warns tourists to Athens in the second century BC, 'there are shysters here that swindle well-to-do strangers who come to town'. Guide books not being readily available, local guides lay in wait. In a satirical sketch, Lucian (second century AD) pictures a tourist examining some paintings in a sanctuary 'and right away two or three people ran up to tell me all about them – for a small fee'. When Cicero, prosecuting Verres, the corrupt Roman governor of Sicily, in 70 BC, had described how Verres had made off with all the art treasures he could find, he went on 'And what about the poor guides who used to make a living showing people round the sites of Syracuse? They had to change their style of operation. Whereas once they showed people where the art treasures were, now they show them where they used to be – before Verres pilfered them.'

Nor would the guides shut up once they had got going. Plutarch (second century AD) tells of a party going round Delphi complaining that the guides 'paid no attention to our entreaties to cut the talk short'. They habitually embroidered their stories – Egyptian guides told tourists that the pyramids extended under the earth as far as they rose above it – and the gullible lapped it up. Pliny the elder is always quoting the bore Mucianus (governor of Syria AD 68) on tall stories he has swallowed, like the elephant that could read and write Greek.

Temples were a major attraction – the museums of the ancient world. One could view the statuary outside just by turning up, but one had to know the opening hours or find the key-holder to view the precious objects kept inside the *cella* (temples were pillaged as ruthlessly as churches). Since sightseers could, as now, grow weary of monuments, locals laid on diversions. On the Nile, priests trained sacred crocodiles to open their mouths and have their teeth cleaned and dried; at Arsinoe, anyone who brought an edible offering to the god Suchus could see the priest call the croc and offer it to him there and then, flushed down with wine. Reigns of terror from drunken crocs roaming the streets are not, however, recorded.

Holiday homes

Apart from the rich, to whom we shall come, most Romans took holidays at home. These were taken during public festivals. Politicians used them to stage cripplingly expensive theatrical spectacles and games: there were votes in slaughtering vast numbers of humans and rare animals. Festivals multiplied, expanded and began to run together. Romans probably worked as little as we do between the *Saturnalia* (December 17-23) and *Compitalia* (January 1-5, complete with first-footing and door decoration). The line was finally drawn at 135 such days a year. Soldiers on campaign were less lucky. They had a right to leave, but secured it only by paying their centurion a steep fee, the *vacatio*. Many spent their leave working to pay for it. Dons on their *vacationes* will hope this practice does not give the education minister ideas.

For the rich, however, Rome was a place to escape from, especially during the stifling summers. Those who sought novel venues in which to escape their cares were rebuked by Stoics like Seneca the younger: for real peace of mind, you must be a different person, not in a different place. But rich Romans mostly retreated to their own or friends' villas. There was only one place to spend the summer – the Bay of Naples (the Roman Cannes), especially to the west (Baiae, perhaps the origin of 'bay') and east (around Sorrento).

Wealthy Romans had been building villas there since the second century BC. By the time of the first emperor Augustus (who ruled 31 BC–AD 14), their multi-storey terraces and piers thrust so far over the water that, as the poet Horace said, even the fish found themselves cramped for space. In the first century BC Cicero, Caesar, Brutus, Pompey and Mark Antony all had villas there: Augustus had four. Vedius Pollio named his villa in Greek *Pausilypon* ('Sans-souci') – it survives today in the name Posillipo. The public servant Pliny the younger (*c.* AD 61-112) was an exception, with only three villas, none in Baiae (one however in Tuscany). He tells us how he writes, walks, exercises, declaims Greek or Latin speeches (to aid digestion) and entertains friends over dinner with talk, readings and recitals. *Plus ça change, plus c'est la même pose.* Today's poetry readings by authors have a long, distinguished history.

Fishing for compliments

While the wealthy nowadays compete in the size of their swimming pools, the Romans did so with their Baiae fishponds, which Lucius Murena ('Eel') invented. Pliny the elder in his *Natural History* is full of useful information on the matter from the first century BC. Lucullus had a channel cut through a mountain to fill his ponds with salt-water (an operation costing more than the villa itself). Pollio was said to feed his stock on human flesh. Gaius Hirrius specialised in lampreys, which became so fashionable that his modest villa + ponds fetched over £1 million. The advocate Hortensius fell so much in love with one partic-ular lamprey that he wept when it died. A neighbour Antonia fitted her favourite lamprey with earrings. Asinius Celer paid £3000 for a mullet.

Cicero called them 'the fishpond set'. The first great fish speculator was Sergius Orata ('Goldfish'). Having made a fortune out of saunas, which every smart villa in the neighbourhood simply had to have, he diversified into oyster-ponds. To sell the product, he announced his oysters from the nearby Lucrine Lake were best of all. Only a late compromise prevented law-suits from oyster-growers elsewhere.

Martial made fun of all this in a poem. The fish in Naples' lakes, he says, are sacred. They recognise and come to lick their lord and master's hand (the emperor's, of course). He gives them names, and they come when summoned. But an ignorant Libyan fisherman once caught one – and was struck blind!

The promenades, the fishponds, the hot springs, and yachting on the lakes around Baiae all offered diversions. At night, things became row-dier ('Why must I look at drunks staggering along the shore or noisy boating parties?' moaned one unhappy holidaymaker) and as Martial said, many a respectable woman 'came to town Penelope [Odysseus' faithful wife], and left it Helen of Troy'. Ibiza has its ancient fore-runners.

Holiday inns

Emperors, however, had to watch it. Absence could be dangerous. Nero frolicked on holiday in AD 68 while the revolt to depose him fomented, and the empire came close to collapse as Tiberius (emperor AD 14-37) saw his time out in his pool on Capri encouraging naked boys to swim between his legs. The Russian President Gorbachev was ejected during his holidays. He should have kept the Roman historians by his bedside.

Travellers today need hotels, but these were, in fact, rare in the ancient world. Aristocrats would stay with friends; those on public business at the special residences built for them on all the major routes; and all the rest at local inns (unless, like St Paul in Rome, you had to stay for some time, when you took a rented room in a private house).

Roman inns were pretty basic, providing food, drink, a bed, stabling for the animals and, often, sex. Names of inns have a familiar ring: The Elephant, The Little Eagle, The Mercury and Apollo. Inns garishly advertised their products and were often decorated with pictures of wine jars or *erotica*. In a poem attributed to the poet Virgil, a lady innkeeper hawks for business on the street, raving about how charming and cool it is inside, advertising the menu, promising the traveller bread, wine and *amor*. Inns would have little in the way of running h. and c. For that, the traveller went to the local baths, which doubled as swimming pool, Turkish bath and general leisure facility. The baths could contain bars, restaurants, gymnasia and beauty salons, and often put on art exhibitions, concerts and lectures. Afterwards, back at his inn, the traveller could eat with everyone else or enjoy room service. Then came the bill. A discussion between innkeeper and guest survives: 'Pint of wine and bread, one *as*. Food, two *asses*.' 'Correct.' 'Girl, eight *asses*.' 'Correct again.' 'Hay for mule, two *asses*.' 'That mule! It'll *ruin* me!'

But one could never be guaranteed a comfortable stay anywhere. Here the Roman philosopher Seneca the younger (AD 1-65) describes what it was like taking rooms over the public baths, the main Roman relaxation facility:

When the muscle men work out with their lead weights and start to strain (or pretend they're straining), you can hear their grunts and then they let out their breath with piercing whistles and wheezes. If someone wants a cheap massage, you can hear the thwack of hands on shoulders, one sort of noise from the flat hand, one from the cupped.

Then a ballplayer arrives and starts counting his shots. At this point I give up. Add the hooligans looking for a fight, the thieves caught in the act and those who sing at the top of their voices in the baths. Add too those who dive into the pool with ear-splitting splashes. On top of all these – who at least make ordinary sounds – there is the hair-removal expert screeching out his services, shutting up only when he's depilating an armpit and someone else is doing the screeching. Then there are people selling drinks, sausages, and cakes, and restaurant owners, all hawking their wares in different tones.

Poor Seneca! Nor was there much rest even when they had all gone home: in many Roman cities it was only at night that heavy-wheeled traffic was allowed on the streets.

Bars and brothels

Romans did not have what we would call restaurants, nor even fast-food shops like McDonald's. They had café-bars and inns. In the bars, drinking was encouraged but not eating (some of the emperors seem to have thought that sitting round a table over dinner led to sedition), and in all-night bars, singing and dancing frequently took over. A fourth-century AD decree from Rome reads: 'No wine shop is to open before 9 am, nobody is to heat water for the public [Romans drank hot water and mixed it with wine], sellers of cooked food can operate only at fixed hours, and no respectable person is to be seen eating in public.' Such decrees probably had not the slightest effect.

Bars often shared a number of characteristics with the inn. Many legal texts class inn-keeping with running a brothel, and any woman who worked in an inn could be assumed to be a prostitute. They were also places where gambling was common (largely illegal, it was never seriously checked). So bars and inns were the big attractions of town over country life. Emperors such as Nero (reigned AD 54-68) were said to patronise them in disguise, revelling the night away and getting into fights (see p. 92). Roman moralists tut-tutted over them incessantly.

Twenty inns and 118 bars have been identified in Pompeii (pop. *c.* 20,000). Many are located in prime spots to attract tourists, like the inn of Euxinus (his name means 'welcoming, hospitable') next to the amphitheatre, with its street corner bar, hot-food counter, wine-racks, back-rooms, lavatory and open-air courtyard, where the drinking, singing, dancing, and gambling probably took place. Euxinus' chums would have regarded McDonald's as a feeble travesty of what a real eating-place should be.

LUCKY STRIKE

Every year the papers reveal the richest person in the world. Whoever it is then usually proclaims that he will 'give it all away'. It is interesting that such people think they have any choice in the matter. Do they imagine they are immortal? But if they try to fulfil their promise, they may find themselves in for a shock. Herodotus tells the following story.

Polycrates (sixth century BC) was the Greek ruler of the island of Samos, just off the coast of modern western Turkey. His navy controlled the eastern Aegean sea. Fabulously wealthy, and with a fine taste for the arts, he indulged in ambitious building projects and invited famous poets of the day to his court. He made an alliance with Amasis, king of Egypt, but Amasis became worried at Polycrates' seemingly endless run of success. So he wrote to him, pointing out that such a run of unbroken luck was bound to end in complete disaster unless he divested himself of the thing he held most precious. Polycrates saw the force of the argument and, selecting a precious ring, sailed out to sea and in front of everyone hurled it into the deep. Six days later, a fisherman arrived at Polycrates' palace to make him a gift of a magnificent fish he had just caught. Polycrates gratefully accepted it, but when the servants cut it up, there was the ring inside. Polycrates at once informed Amasis of what had happened. Convinced Polycrates was doomed, Herodotus tells us, Amasis broke off the alliance.

In fact, it was Polycrates who broke off the alliance because he realised that Amasis was about to be defeated by the king of Persia, and Polycrates knew whose side he would rather be on. But Herodotus has a point to make, and goes on to make it. In 522 BC, he says, Polycrates was lured into a trap, gruesomely murdered and his body hung on a cross. Polycrates *was* doomed, after all – and Amasis had been right all along.

Rich irony

It is a commonplace of ancient Greek thought that happiness is both elusive and illusory, and that great prosperity goes hand in hand with imminent disaster. It is the very heart of tragedy, invented by Greeks, that a person of apparent blessedness should suddenly be brought low. The classic example again comes from Herodotus.

King Croesus of Lydia (western Turkey, d. 546 BC) was one of the richest men in the world. One day the Athenian wise man Solon visited Croesus and Croesus, knowing his reputation, sent him on a guided tour of his treasuries and then asked him who was the happiest man in the world, 'supposing the answer would be himself'. Solon replied that it was the Athenian Tellus, all of whose children and grandchildren survived, who had enough wealth, and who, dying gloriously in battle, received a public funeral. Miffed, Croesus asked for the runner-up and was told Cleobis and Biton. These two young prize-winning athletes from Argos, finding that their mother needed to be taken to the sanctuary of Hera five miles away but that the oxen had not arrived in time, got between the shafts themselves and pulled her there (you can still see Argos from the Hera sanctuary). Everyone congratulated them, and their mother prayed that Hera would reward them with whatever was best for a human. When the rituals were over, Cleobis and Biton lay down to rest in the temple and never awoke (their statues are in the museum at Delphi).

'But what about *me*?', whined Croesus. Solon's magnificent reply pointed out that 'the god is envious of human prosperity and disruptive ... and man is entirely a creature of chance'. Croesus might appear to be rich and rule many people, but 'I will not answer your question until I know that you have died happily. Great wealth can make a man no happier than moderate means, unless he has the luck to remain prosperous to the end ... So until a man is dead, keep the word "happy" in reserve. Till then he is not happy, merely lucky ... Look to the end, no matter what you are considering. Often enough the god gives a man a glimpse of happiness and then utterly uproots him.'

Croesus dismisses Solon for a fool: how could he possibly ask him to look to the end of all things, when his present prosperity was so great? Herodotus goes on 'But when Solon had left, great retribution from the god seized Croesus, in all likelihood because he reckoned himself to be the most happy of men'. His best-loved son was killed in a hunting accident, and Croesus himself was captured by Cyrus the Persian, bound and placed on a funeral pyre to be burnt to death. As he stood there, helpless, he called on the name of Solon three times. Asked on whom he was calling, he replied 'Someone whom I would give a fortune to have every ruler in the world meet'.

For 'ruler' read, perhaps, multi-millionaire.

ATOMIC DEATH

People today believe all diseases, even old age, should be curable. Doctors seem to treat death as medical failure. It is as if people think they should be immortal – or are terrified of dying. Amidst all the research, however, the laboratory mice retain a commendably stoic silence.

Perhaps the mice have all read Lucretius. In book 3 of his stunning *de rerum natura* ('On the Nature of the Universe'), he argues that the soul is mortal, and eloquently denounces as fools those who fear death. Lucretius is an atomist and follower of the Greek philosopher Epicurus, and sees body, mind and soul as composed of matter. This matter is very fine, consisting of the tiniest imaginable atomic particles, and thinly spread throughout the body. When we die, this matter disentangles itself from us, breaks down into its component atoms and dissipates into thin air like smoke. Mind and soul, being atomic, are dissipated too, and return to join the great individual atom pool that makes up the universe.

Consequently, Lucretius goes on, death is nothing to us and no concern of ours. He rehearses what Nature would say about it: 'Why weep over death? If life till now has been pleasant enough, why not leave it as a guest who has eaten their fill, carefree at heart? But if life has become disagreeable, why continue with it?' He concludes: 'Life is given on freehold to no one; to all, it is on lease. Past generations had trodden your path: so too will future. Reflect on the eternity that passed before we came into this world, and see how utterly it counts for nothing. Nature holds the past up to us as a mirror, where we can see what that time will be like when we are dead.'

The same argument applies to the cloning issue, scientists having now artificially cloned one sheep from another (a cloned animal is produced asexually and has its parent's identical genetic make-up – unlike identical twins, which have the same genetic make-up as each other). What if they start doing the same to humans, especially cloning the living from the dead? Lucretius sees the point, and asks 'What if the atoms that made us up should be reassembled by time' (he might have added 'or by scientists') 'after our death and returned to what they were?' But he has an answer: 'Even that would still be of no relevance to us once the chain of our identity had been broken. We who live now have no connection with ourselves in any earlier incarnation ... someone who no longer exists cannot be any different from someone who has never been born.'

Ancient Greeks, with their passion for knowledge (see p. 42), would have loved the idea that we shall soon know the sequence and approximate functions of all 80,000 human genes, and therefore be in a better position to control our lives (though we are nowhere near understanding the fantastically complex workings of the brain). What they would reject, however, is the idea that this knowledge should be the means by which our lives should *be* controlled. Science, for them, would be their slave, not their master. Choice about what to do with all the ramifications of this knowledge would remain with the chooser, not with scientists, doctors or bureaucrats.

Dead powerful

Lucretius was fighting a losing battle then (and fights it still). There were as many ancient views about death and the after-life as there were people prepared to discuss it, all the way from eighth-century BC Homer (for whom it was a dull, grey, boring shadow of the vigorous, energetic, heroic, competitive life on earth) to third-century AD philosophers like Porphyry who thought of the soul mystically returning to The One (and not eating meat, to help it on its way). One particularly powerful train of ancient thought related to the power of the dead over the living (see p. 162), which survives into the modern world. One remembers the extended odyssey of the embalmed corpse of Eva Perón, wife of the Argentinian dictator Juan. Dying in 1952, she was shunted off as far as Italy by terrified opponents before finally returning to Buenos Aires in 1971.

Anyone who died 'before their time', for example, was thought to roam the earth till the 'right' time had come. So someone with a grudge against X would deposit a 'curse tablet' in the grave of the early dead, a strip of lead ordering the dead person to roam the earth, find X, and make life hell. In the Christian era, saints' bodies were deeply vener-ated. They were endowed with enormous powers for good. Their presence both protected a place and attracted the lucrative pilgrim market with hopes of a miracle. So they were frequently stolen and relocated – St Mark from Alexandria (in a pork barrel to put off the Muslim customs inspectors) to Venice in the ninth century AD, St Nicholas (Santa Claus) from Myra (Turkey) to Bari (Italy) in the eleventh. The body of Alexander the Great, who died in Babylon in 323 BC after taking his army as far east as India, was also hijacked. He wanted to be buried at Siwah in Egypt, home of the oracle of Zeus-Ammon which had proclaimed him a son of Zeus, but Ptolemy, the Greek ruler of Alexandria in Egypt, was having none of that. He had the body diverted to Alexandria, where it was put on grand display and visited by the great and good for centuries (including the Roman emperor Augustus). This attitude to the dead may be a reason why one of the few questions asked of an Athenian who wanted to stand for public office was whether he had tended the family grave (see p. 75). One could not have a public official with a dead man's curse hanging over him.

Old theorem

None of this, however, prevented the ancients from developing a theory of old age and how to endure it. The modern world is obsessed by the ageing process and anti-ageism is rife (in the USA, absurdly, one cannot be forcibly retired because one is old). The biblical patriarchs would probably have approved. Adam lived to 930 and Methuselah held the record at 969 before God cut the natural span to 120. Even they were striplings, however, compared with the early Sumerian kings (modern Iraq), of whom En Men Lu Anna clocked in at a pension-busting 43,200.

But for an ancient Greek or Roman, getting over fifty was the problem. The combined dangers of childbirth, disease, diet and war meant that death rates peaked at birth, early childhood and the twenties. Those who made it into their thirties might expect another twenty years. The possible life-span, however, was as today: we have records of Greeks living to 100 (usually philosophers, inevitably).

One result of the compression of the life-span was that Greeks had virtually no concept of middle age. One was 'young' up till 30, then 'old'. The Greek philosopher Pythagoras (sixth century BC) went even further, dividing life into four stages – 0-20 childhood; 20-40 adolescence; 40-60 youth; 60-80 old age. This is very sensible: tied to the cult of Yoof as we are today, we do ourselves no favours at all with a concept of 'middle age' that usually turns into a period of 'trauma' and 'searching for one's real self', with usually hilarious and often disastrous results. But as more and more couples avoid children till as late as possible, it may be that 20-40 is becoming a kind of prolonged adolescence, while the 40-60's increasingly seem to burst with life and vigour (all that ghastly keeping fit). Perhaps we are entering the age of Pythagoras.

Mixed blessings

As for the experience of old age, it was desirable in principle to live long, but old age was also feared. A terrifying Greek myth makes the point well. Eous ('Dawn'), immortal wife of mortal Tithonus, wanted her husband to live for ever, and her wish was granted. But she forgot to ask for eternal youth for him, and he faded agonisingly away, quite unable to die. Old age was regularly described as 'hateful' and 'painful', and Aristotle offered some scathing arguments against it: oldies are 'positive about nothing, lacking in drive, always looking on the worst side of everything, suspicious, small-minded, mean (they know from experience how hard it is to get property and how easy to lose it)' and so on. Cephalus at the start of Plato's *Republic* (*c.* 375 BC) claims old age may bring respect, but people complain, he says, of its loss of vigour. Cephalus thinks it is character that counts: then it does not matter what age you are. The fifth-century tragedian Sophocles evidently agreed that one of the greatest blessings of old age was freedom from the sexual urge, which hounded one like a tyrannical master a slave.

The most famous treatise on the subject is Cicero's brilliant *de senectute* ('On Old Age', 44 BC). Old age, inevitably, was more admired in oligarchies like Rome than democracies like Athens ('Senate' derives from *senex*, 'old man'), but it still had to be handled. Cicero discusses the four objections to it: it removes us from active work, weakens the body, deprives us of physical pleasure, and brings us close to death. He deals with each in turn, emphasising the power that derives from the development of experience and wisdom, and the pleasure and advantage inherent in adapting to nature's ways as the years pass: 'the old will be respected only if they fight for themselves, maintain their own rights, avoid dependence, and assert their authority over their households as long as life lasts'. Faced wisely, old age is a great blessing, enabling us to approach death naturally, like a man nearing harbour after a long voyage – catching sight of land at last.

So Cicero would have had hard things to say about the new sex-drug Viagra. In *de senectute*, he argues that blind lust 'clouds a man's judgement, obstructs his capacity for reasoning and dulls his intelligence' and that one of the pleasures of old age is that, while it is not wholly deficient in sensual pleasures, it does not miss them – and so cannot be said to lack them. Consequently, the weakening of temptation to indulge in them, far from supplying an excuse to inveigh against old age, is actually a reason for offering old age hearty congratulations. Cicero goes on to point out that, when an Athenian thinker (Epicurus, 341-271 BC) asserted that pleasure was the standard by which everything should be judged, the Roman reaction was to pray that their Greek enemies embraced this doctrine – they would be a walkover.

Cicero continues in the vein of the Preacher, that to everything there is a season, and a time to every purpose under the heaven. 'Boys have their own typical pursuits, but adolescents do not hanker after them because they have their own interests. These in their turn cease to attract mature grown ups because they too have their special interests – for which, when their time comes, the old feel no desire since they again, finally, have interests peculiar to themselves. Then, like earlier occupations, these activities fall away; and when that happens, a man has had enough of life and it is time to die.' In this most servile of ages, where dependence on resources impersonal to oneself has never been greater – those provided by government and media like television being far more mind-sapping than drugs – Viagra is yet another invitation to self-enslavement. Ancients, by the way, would have greeted with contempt the 'tragic' sob-stories endlessly commissioned by newspapers about 'stars' who 'yielded to' or 'finally beat' drugs or drink, as if they deserved sympathy or applause. There was a time when the weak-willed, easily-led and slavish were not objects of universal admiration: ancients would have seen nothing 'tragic' about them at all.

And so to bed

Society today makes inordinate efforts to prevent the young having children while at the same time encouraging the old to live as long as possible (the government has been refusing even the consolation of death by T-bone steak to see us oldies out). So it is not surprising that we have such problems with e.g. public pension schemes. One solution would be thoroughly Roman – telling people to commit suicide (perhaps with the guarantee of a posthumous honour or a tax-rebate for relatives). But death was never a problem for those of Stoic disposition (see p. 160), as the Roman millionaire poet, thinker and public figure Seneca (adviser to Nero) makes clear.

In a letter to a friend Seneca writes of a mutual acquaintance, Tullius Marcellinus, 'who began to contemplate suicide after he had gone down with a disease which was not incurable but was still protracted and difficult'. Various friends are summoned to give advice, the timid suggesting he should do whatever he wanted, the flatterers trying to gratify him – no one, in other words, giving any genuine thought to his condition. A Stoic philosopher then arrives. He points out, first, that living *per se* is no particularly great thing: even animals and slaves do it. Nor, therefore, is dying. What is a great thing, however, is to die 'in a manner which is honourable, enlightened and courageous'.

Marcellinus needs no second bidding. His slaves refuse to help, until the Stoic points out that they are in no danger since their master's death is a voluntary one; besides, it is just as bad for a slave to refuse to do his master's bidding as actually to kill him. Marcellinus therefore refuses food. He has a steam tent put up in his bedroom and his bath filled with continual supplies of hot water in which he almost imperceptibly fades away, frequently commenting on the pleasurable sensation this induces, 'rather like fainting'.

Seneca goes on to draw the moral: 'we need such examples. Too often we cannot reconcile ourselves to dying, or to knowing it is time to die.' He points out that slavery is the most abject condition, and that the person who fears death is nothing better than a slave – 'for life itself is slavery if we lack the courage to die'. To those who argue they still have duties to perform, Seneca points out that dying is one of life's duties, and ends with a fine image: 'in this respect life is like a play – what is important is not the length of the performance, but how good it is ... make sure you round it off with a good ending.' Now watch out for the Health Secretary banning hot baths.

Herodotus tells us that the Massagetae (in modern Turkmen) did it all automatically by imposing a maximum old age. On reaching it, the oldie was sacrificed by relatives, boiled and eaten. Such a death was regarded as 'most blessed'. Now there's a thought.

2

Science, Argument and Medicine

Fossils buried in a meteorite originating from Mars recently suggested to some that there may once have been life on that planet, which could also have been the source of life on earth. Early Greek philosophers of the sixth century BC would have been thrilled. Not, however, Socrates.

The first Greek philosophers, like Thales and Anaximander, all 'students of nature' as Aristotle called them, were like natural scientists. They wanted to know what the *real* nature of things, their essence or fundamental properties, was. So they set out to describe the universe's origin and workings. On the one hand they gave accounts of natural phenomena like stars, planets, weather, plants, animals and man; on the other they raised what we would call philosophical questions about whether and how the universe began, what it was made of, why it changed and so on. They were the first people we know of to argue that the world did not run on some irrational, divine whim but was logically ordered, systematic, and therefore fully comprehensible in human, not supernatural, terms. Argument and evidence were for them the keystones to understanding. Since they could not get below the level of perception and therefore had to argue purely from what they could see, most of their premises, and so conclusions, were false, but the principles of reasoning from evidence marked the beginning of genuinely scientific thought.

For example, they argued about what single substance the world consisted of. Earth, air, water and fire were all proposed. But that created another problem: if everything was 'air', how did it become e.g. wood or blood? They solved this problem of change by inventing the atomic theory: that the basic substance was too small to detect, but its combination in different shapes, sizes and textures created the world we see.

Proper study

Socrates (469-399 BC) changed all that. He was captivated by this sort of speculation when young, but in time he came to see how empty its debates were (e.g. when you add one to one, does the first or second become two, or do they both become two?) because it did not seem to him to address the really important questions – what are we here for and why? Or, to put it another way, how best should we live? He reached the conclusion that happiness consisted not in worldly success but goodness, and that if only we knew what goodness was we would always do it. His disciple Plato tried to solve the problem of knowing what goodness was with reference to his famous theory of Forms, i.e. that this world is somehow merely a pale, shadowy reflection of another, higher world of true knowledge to which we can aspire only through the most intense philosophical commitment.

So Socrates would have wondered why billions of dollars were about to be spent on fossils, when so many human questions remain unresolved. He would have become interested only when scientists could produce a real live Martian for him to ask what goodness was.

Royal strife

One particularly interesting 'pre-Socratic' philosopher was Heraclitus (c. 500 BC). His theory of opposites was picked up in a recent VE day address by Prince Charles, who talked about the 'paradoxical nature of our earthly existence – that everything consists of opposites ... good and evil, death and life'. Heraclitus was trying to explain the problem of change, and argued that fire was the basic stuff common to everything, including the human soul, and this caused things to change (after all, fire does change things). Further, he argued that all changes were regular and balanced. Thus day changed into and was balanced by night (and *vice versa*), as did winter and summer, war and peace, and so on. Indeed, the world existed only because of this constant process of change: 'everything is in a state of flux', he famously said. The world, then, consisted of oppositions, but it was still a unity. For example, Heraclitus said, 'the path up and down is one and the same' – a path goes up, seen from one point of view, and down, seen from another, but it is still one path: 'up' and 'down' are essentially the same thing.

Prince Charles ended his speech by saying that we could reach 'inner peace' by trying to reconcile opposites. Heraclitus would have disagreed: only unending 'strife' between opposites maintained the unity of the universe.

Atomic expense

The atomic theory of the universe – that it was made up of 'atoms' (*atomoi*, Greek for 'uncuttables'), unchanging, indivisible particles below the level of perception – was first proposed by Leucippus and Democritus (fifth century BC). The universe, they argued, was formed by these atoms moving randomly through empty space and crashing into each other. This set up whirlpools of atoms, which bunched together into 'lumps' of matter.

The Greek thinker Epicurus took up the theory, but saw a problem. It was agreed that atoms, falling through empty space, must fall at the same speed. But then the universe would be 'smooth': the atoms would not be able to crash into each other and start clustering together to form 'lumps' of matter. The solution Epicurus came up with is his famous theory of the 'atomic swerve' – that any atom, unpredictably, could swerve, knock into another atom, and generate the 'lumps'.

The ancients mocked this: they did not believe in causeless motion. Quite right too. Modern cosmologists have now (to their great relief, though at vast cost) identified evidence of a ripple at an early enough stage to have given the universe time enough to move out of a 'smooth' and into a 'lumpy' state and form the universe we know.

Lacking modern technology, ancient scientists were armchair thinkers, convinced a rational universe would yield its secret to pure thought, and oddly indifferent to testing their conclusions by even simple experiment. Believing the universe was basically simple, they set about explaining its complexity. Modern cosmologists agree, and in an age which grovels so abjectly at the shrine of 'use' and 'economy', the exquisite uselessness and staggering expense of such research are equally cheering.

Stars in their eyes

Even astrology was brought into the net of ancient reason. Astrology rests upon foundations laid by Babylonians and enlarged by Greeks, Romans and Arabs. President Reagan, we are told, even used it to help shape policy – a most sensible move, given the alternative. But if astrology is basically ham psychology with a little cosmic mysticism thrown in to give the feeble-minded a thrill, how is it that even Greeks such as the great philosopher Aristotle swallowed it?

Ancient astronomers knew enough about the heavens to be able to contrast the unchanging regularity of their movement with the chaos of life on earth. From there it was a short step to argue that the heavens were divine. If so, they must exert some influence upon the earth. But how? Two assumptions underpinned the answer. First, Greeks believed that the world consisted of four basic elements – earth, air, fire and water – roughly representing heat, dryness and moisture (see p. 52). Different mixtures of these produced change in the world. Second, on the strength of their limited observations, they postulated a cosmos in which the seven planets that they could see (including the sun and the moon, but not Uranus, Neptune or Pluto) shifted position against the background of the twelve signs of the zodiac. So by analogy with the effect of the sun and moon on e.g. tides, seasons, etc., and a general belief in 'cosmic sympathy', they argued that the fluctuating relationship between planet and zodiac generated different mixtures of heat, cold, dryness and moisture in the world. So the heavens *did* affect life on earth, and the predictability of the heavens ensured the predictability of life.

Twaddle, of course. But the point is that the ancients at least tried to produce a rational account of their beliefs which accorded with their understanding of the world. With the whole of twentieth-century science at their disposal, modern astrologers' accounts are doubtless far more powerful.

Problem pages

The ceaselessly curious ancient Greeks were also pretty good at the Note-and-Query. This genre, in which readers are invited to send in questions to newspapers to be answered either by a resident expert or other readers, is not as modern as we think it is.

Pseudo-Aristotle got there first over two thousand years ago with his *Problems* (in 38 books), and Plutarch (c. AD 46-120) followed hot on his heels with his *Roman Questions*. In both cases, a question is put, usually beginning 'Why is it that …?', to which the answer is given 'Is it because …?'. The formidable brows of our most famous agony aunts could find themselves beetling at some of these ancient posers, such as 'Why is the year unhealthy in which there is a large supply of small, toad-like frogs?', 'Why does everything appear to the very drunk to be going round in circles?', 'Why is it that bare feet are not good for sexual intercourse?', 'Why is it difficult to walk up a steep hill?', 'Why is it easier to hear in the night than during the day?', 'Why do those who are blind from birth never go bald?', 'Why is sneezing between midnight and midday not a good thing?', and 'Why do male sex maniacs' eyes and buttocks sink inwards?'

Questions to be answered

The answers fill anything from one line to several pages. Thus 'Why do men sneeze more than any other animal?' probes Ps-Aristotle. 'Is it because he has wide channels through which breath and smell enter?' Very likely. 'Why do fishermen have sandy hair?' Ps-Aristotle argues it is something to do with salt and the drying properties of the sun. 'Why, when the east wind blows, does everything seem larger?' Ps-Aristotle thinks it may be because an east wind 'makes everything very gloomy'. Marks for originality, at least. 'Why have animals an even number of feet?' The Psage reckons this is because when anything moves, something must be at rest – so feet are arranged in pairs. Good thinking! 'Why is it that the very drunk do not behave badly, but the slightly drunk do?' Possibly because the slightly drunk are still able to exercise judgement, but poorly, opines the Ps-philosopher shrewdly.

And so it goes on. 'Why do leeks assist clear speech?' 'Why do sex maniacs' eyelashes fall out?' Excellent questions, all of them. If the answers are only rarely enlightening, it is important to understand that Greeks, however 'rational', could not be properly scientific – it is the old story of false assumptions and so, inevitably, wrong conclusions. Still, it is the principle that counts. It says something that these questions were asked in the first place, let alone that it was felt they could be answered.

It is indeed difficult to underestimate Greek curiosity and their desire for mastery over knowledge. When Alexander the Great (taught by Aristotle) went on his epic march from Greece almost to Karachi and back to Babylon where he died in 323 BC, he took with him historians and philosophers as well as navigators, guides, and surveyors. Moreover, we are told, he ordered thousands of people throughout Greece and Asia who made their living by hunting, fowling, fishing, bee-keeping and so on to make sure that 'Aristotle should not remain ignorant of any animal born anywhere'.

SPEAKING UP FOR DEMOCRACY

Enoch Powell was once voted by Radio 4 listeners the country's best user of the English language. Since Mr Powell was a politician, the ancients would have found the choice entirely credible, since politics in the ancient world was all about oratory, i.e. public speech-making.

Rhetoric, the rules for delivering effective, persuasive oratory, was said to have been invented by Teisias and Korax, two Greeks living in Sicily, around 470 BC. The timing of its invention is highly significant. Democracy had been invented in Athens in 507 BC (p. 72), and in the

470s cities in Sicily were in the process of moving from tyranny to democracy. In other words, rhetoric and democracy went hand-in-hand (see pp. 52, 76).

The reason is that Athenian democracy involved *all* male citizens over 18 in making decisions about their city. Since decisions were taken on the strength of public debate in the Assembly, everyone had to be given the chance to develop successful speaking skills: otherwise, the democracy ran the risk of becoming the plaything of the naturally articulate, with the rest of the people nowhere. So during the fifth century BC we begin to hear of the production in Athens of handbooks of persuasive arguments; and private teachers of rhetoric sprang up, called 'sophists', who offered classes in the subject for a fee. This art of peaceful persuasion was not just important in itself (Greeks thought there were three techniques for getting your way – persuasion, force and trickery); it enabled everyone both to use it and (just as important) know when it was being used.

Plato was against it. Teaching people the means of effective persuasion could be justified only if the end in view was good. So while Plato might have applauded Mr Powell's rhetorical technique, he would have thought it more important to ask 'What is he being rhetorical *about?*'

Rhetorical questions

Modern politicians, having no time for genuine democracy, hate being asked to justify their policies and always moan about the way they are treated by the public media. But help is at hand for them, in the shape of Aristotle. It was he who produced the first full analysis of the 'means of persuasion' in his *Art of Rhetoric* and turned persuasiveness into a systematic and almost scientific enterprise. Romans such as Cicero (106-43 BC) and Quintilian (*c.* AD 35-95) followed suit, building on and refining the Greek models.

It was not just a matter of stylistic devices or speech structure. Aristotle contrasted 'non-artistic' means of persuasion, like written documents, with 'artistic', of which three were commonly identified: the presentation of the character of the speaker (honest, trustworthy); the arousal of favourable emotional responses in the audience; and the use of arguments (Aristotle invented the syllogism for this purpose). These included arguments from induction, deduction, and probability ('is it *likely* that X would have done this?'). It was also important to determine what you were trying to prove. Cases were best made by arguing that a course of action was just, or beneficial, or appropriate, or honourable. Each demanded a different type of approach. All this could be defined, systematised, and learned. But the ancients failed to come up with an adequate answer to the most important problem of all: ensuring a speech was perfectly attuned to time, place and audience. No theory could prevent all sorts of unforeseen distractions distorting the reception of the message. MPs were unwise, for example, to spread their cheering message among holiday-makers on the beach, as some did a few years ago. Few get pleasure out of beach-balls.

All politicians have to do, then, is discover what is just, beneficial, appropriate or honourable about their policy, and attune it to the psychology of the British electorate. On reflection, one can see why they prefer to blame the media.

In opposition: education vs. training

One of the main weaknesses of ancient Greek argument was its inclination to see everything in terms of opposites – body/soul, mind/matter, black/white, male/female, and so on. The very fact of deploying them suggested that they could not reconciled. Three famous oppositions ring down the ages. The first is that between the vocational and the non-vocational.

It was Isocrates, an Athenian orator and professor of education of the fourth century BC, who first asserted the superiority of the vocational. Isocrates taught rhetoric, but today he would have called it 'communication skills' in order to impress businessmen. Isocrates was a vocationist, and he contrasted himself with his rivals such as Plato and other philosophers, the theorists of the day. These people, he argued, despised vocational skills like rhetoric and were interested only in *abstract* truth. In what looks like a brochure advertising his own teaching aims and objectives, he condemns them as follows: 'they ought to abandon this claptrap, which pretends to prove things by verbal quibbles, and to pursue truth and instruct their pupils in the practical affairs of government: for probability in what is useful is far preferable to exactness in what is not'.

The philosophers' answer was that communication skills were merely the means to ends and consequently could actually do harm if the ends were wicked (with reason: we are all aware of the consequences of glossy 'communicating' aimed at persuading us to e.g. borrow more money than we can afford). Consequently, they argued, only the philosopher, knowing the distinction between right and wrong, could be trusted with such a potentially deadly means as rhetoric. Philosophy, or theory, must therefore come first, rhetoric later.

Underridable

The second ancient opposition that continues to give trouble is that between absolutists and relativists – those who believe there is such a thing as 'truth' and those who do not. Firmly in the relativist camp are literary deconstructionists like the French imposter Jacques Derrida. The honorary degree he received from Cambridge in 1992 was really a posthumous degree to the great Greek thinker from Abdera (in North-Eastern Greece) Protagoras (c. 490-420 BC).

Protagoras said: 'Man is the measure of all things, of things that are, as to how they are, and of things that are not, as to how they are not.' The ancients understood by this: if honey seems sweet to some and bitter to others, then that is what it *is*.

This raises a problem. If individuals are the measure of all things in this way, we cannot say whether honey is *objectively* sweet or bitter. It just depends who is tasting it at the time. But if so, we cannot say anyone's perception of anything is false: honey seems sweet to me, but if it seems bitter to Bloggs, bitter to Bloggs it is. The conclusion that springs from this is devastating: everyone's perception of things *must* be true. Further, Bloggs and I are not contradicting each other in the matter of the taste of honey. (My experience is mine, Bloggs's is Bloggs's.) There is no objective reality about the taste of honey *to* contradict.

The argument is unimportant in relation to honey, but transfer it to issues of right and wrong, good and bad, fair and foul and we are in serious trouble. Is morality relative, a matter of individual perceptions? Must everyone, by definition, be 'right' about it? Derrida, with his views on the meaninglessness of words and impossibility of constructing a definitive statement about anything, is simply a child of Protagoras, and a painfully unoriginal one at that.

This presented a real challenge to the brilliant Cambridge Public Orator Professor James Diggle, who had to construct a speech in Latin in Derrida's honour for the honorary degree ceremony. Diggle was up to it, elegantly saying how brilliant the old fraud was in an *oratio* in which he emphasised Derrida's theory that *oratio* tells one nothing. Did Derrida get it? Of course not. He grinned contentedly away while his deconstructionist chums all clapped like circus sea-lions.

Spelling rite

The third famous opposition involves the question whether there is
any right and wrong in the use of language (a recent series of Reith lectures was dedicated to the subject). One of the most successful
exponents of the anti-liberal line in the ancient world was the second-
century AD grammarian Apollonius Dyscolus ('the grouch').
Apollonius took against 'those who say there is no right and wrong in
such matters, and assume that [linguistic] phenomena have all been
established by chance, as unconnected'.

Apollonius argued that if (for example) you examined traditional
orthography, you could see that there were historical reasons behind
word-formation and spelling. These generated rules, that could then be
learned. As a result, it was possible to identify spelling errors and correct them. If there were no rules, one could not do that.

The same, Apollonius argued, applied to every aspect of language. If
you examined the whole tradition of language usage, you could see it
was governed by rules, and rules could be applied, and 'right' and
'wrong' usage therefore established. Exceptions, as ever, simply proved
that rules existed – otherwise how could you tell they were exceptions?

There is obviously much in this. Clearly, if there were no rules about
how language worked, it would be impossible for people to communicate at all. Further, such a discipline as linguistics would not exist, since,
if language were truly random, nothing could be said about it. If, however, the concept of an imposed, standard English seems tyrannical,
consider in fact how democratic it is – giving everyone equal access to
universally agreed and understood norms. How different than/from/to
liberal chaos!

Prof scoff

Plato was utterly opposed to everything that relativists such as
Protagoras stood for. In one of his dialogues Plato elegantly takes him
off, describing how the Great Thinker descends on Athens, complete
with admiring retinue. Socrates' young friend Hippocrates is terribly
excited at the prospect and begs Socrates for an introduction. He wants
to learn how to be wise, but Socrates is dubious – what sort of wisdom
is it that Protagoras claims to impart? Still, he accompanies the youth
to Callias's house, where Protagoras and the other mighty brains are
staying.

They have some trouble with Callias's doorman, who is fed up with all these bleedin' intellectuals crowding out the place, but are finally admitted. Socrates describes how Protagoras is walking up and down in the portico, with a long line of worshippers in tow 'following spell-bound, charmed by his Orpheus-like voice ... I was delighted to see what care they took never to get in front or be in Protagoras' way. When he turned round, the listeners divided this way and that, executing a circular movement which took them to their places in the rear again. Beautiful!'

Socrates now lists further devotees, and mentions that, such was the press of intellectuals, the great Prodicus had to be put up in a lumber-room, where he still lay in bed, well wrapped up. Sadly, Socrates reports, he could not hear what Prodicus was saying, much though he wanted to: 'he has such a deep voice that there was a kind of booming noise in the room, which drowned his words.' Naughty Socrates! Such irony directed at the world of the star intellectual.

Empathy sympathy

Today's school history syllabus is dominated by 'empathy', i.e. encouraging children to use their imaginations to think their way into the minds of historical figures, whether they actually know anything about them or not. Interestingly, this was the standard method Romans developed for teaching effective oratory.

Such exercises were called *suasoriae* and were at the heart of the Romans' higher education system. Students were given a problem, usually from ancient Greek or Roman myth or history, and told to construct the pros and cons of a character solving it in one or another way. Should Agamemnon sacrifice his daughter in order to gain the wind that will take the fleet to Troy and start the Trojan war? Should Socrates drink the hemlock? Should Hannibal march on Rome after defeating the Romans at the battle of Cannae? Should Cicero try to save his life by agreeing to burn all his books?

This was all very career-oriented. A Roman aristocrat (at whom this education was directed) would normally be looking to carve out a life in government or the law, where the ability to speak persuasively was the key to success. The more practice he received in arguing difficult or unlikely cases, the better. Roman style 'empathy' exercises, then, are well-suited to modern education, where knowing things does not really count for much, but high-gloss 'communication skills' – never mind what it is you are communicating – will open all doors.

ANIMAL CRACKERS

Every year in the summer, convoys of 'travellers' hit the road, proclaiming their 'alternative' life-styles. Diogenes the 'Cynic' (400-325 BC), father of them all, would have had nothing but contempt for them.

A contemporary of the philosophers Plato and Aristotle, Diogenes had no interest in logic, science or metaphysics. Believing real human nature to be primitive and animal-like, he rejected all ties of family and nationality and flouted all conventions and standards of behaviour. He lived (it seemed) with all the shamelessness of a dog (Greek stem *kun-*, whence 'cynic'). In Athens he lived in a large earthenware jar. Alexander the Great visited him and offered him anything he wanted. 'Stand out of my light' came the reply. When Plato defined 'man' as a featherless biped, Diogenes came into class with a plucked chicken, saying 'Here is Plato's man'. He declared the love of money to be the 'metropolis' of all evils. He wrote an *Oedipus* and an *Atreus*, highlighting points in favour of incest and cannibalism. Plato described him as 'Socrates gone potty'.

This prolific author (nothing, alas, survives), preacher and iconoclast did resemble Socrates in that he believed happiness to be unconnected with worldly goods, but dependent rather on inner resources that could be nurtured only by severe physical and mental self-discipline. Self-sufficiency, freedom of speech, indifference to hardship and lack of shame were Cynic hallmarks. Such extremism was attractive (it is the nearest the ancient world got to mendicant friars) but it easily degenerated into exhibitionist beggary. The ancients knew the difference. Of today's 'travellers', little better than putty in the hands of the billionaire pop-market, Diogenes would have replied as he did when he was asked if there was a great crowd at the Olympic games: 'Yes, a great crowd, but few that could be called men.'

Diogenes' contention that we were 'really' rather primitive animals was strongly contested by the ancients. No ancient thought we were animal in origin, even Anaximander (610-545 BC). He reasoned that, because babies were so helpless, we must have had some kind of protection in our primitive state; and he speculated that we emerged from the sea preserved in a sort of fish-like shell, out of which we burst, fully formed. His guess that we have our origins in the sea is a brilliant one, but he did not think we were 'fish' in any sense.

As for behaviour, while ancient Greeks agreed that man did behave 'naturally' (i.e. like animals) in some respects, it was human *nomoi* ('laws', 'customs', 'tradition') that separated us from beasts. So, for example, it was 'natural' to have children, but 'custom' to expect them to repay parents for their trouble. Greeks pinpointed as especially distinctive our powers of reasoning, our ability to create agreeable living conditions, and our formation of communities with laws to curb aggression (they also far-sightedly reflected that we created problems for ourselves that nature alone never could). So ancient Greeks, faced with the claim that we were 'really' animals, would look at our laws, customs and traditions to see if they distinctively differentiated us from animals or not. They probably still do – just.

Animal magic

Not that ancients necessarily disrespected animals. The philosopher Porphyry (third century AD) produced a range of arguments for vegetarianism, believing animate food was bad for the soul. The Greek moral philosopher and historian Plutarch devotes a whole treatise to them, entitled 'On the Cleverness of Animals'.

This essay takes the form of a dialogue, and the six speakers first establish that animals are rational because they e.g. plan for the future, have memory, care for their young, show gratitude and can be courageous and big-hearted. Then, using hundreds of examples, they debate whether land or sea animals are superior. Aristotimus argues for land animals. Dogs put pebbles into a half-empty jar to bring the liquid to the top for drinking. Geese flying through eagles' territory carry stones in their beaks so they do not give themselves away by honking. Then what of the dim circus elephant, who, tired of being punished for forgetting his tricks, practised by moonlight to get them right? Cows in Persia can count: they lift a hundred buckets of water a day to irrigate the king's park – but not one more.

Phaedimus replies for marine animals. Fish must be brainy, being almost uncatchable. Sacred crocodiles in Egypt recognise the priests' voices when they call, and open their mouths to have their teeth cleaned. Tunny fish are experts in optics and maths: having weak right eyes, they always keep their left eye to seaward to watch out for danger, and they feed in schools formed into perfect six-sided cubes. Dolphins have rescued countless humans from the sea. And so on and on and on …

Bangs and whimpers

Ancients as a whole had few compunctions about killing humans, let alone animals (hunting was a fine, healthy pastime, blessed by the gods). But while environmental pollution is nothing new (the younger Seneca notices how different he feels in the country when he has left Rome with its 'reek of smoking cookers, its cloud of ashes and poisonous fumes') it was localised. Our present, world-wide pollution would have met with the strongest moral and religious condemnation.

The reason is that ancients had a general belief that the world was divine and eternal. There was a strong sense of the sacredness of the earth, mother Gaia, one of the earliest of gods. For some thinkers, this meant that man was a stranger here on earth; for others, like the unceasingly curious encyclopaedist Pliny the elder (killed investigating the eruption of Vesuvius that buried Pompeii, AD 79), it meant man and nature were one, and that nature's purpose was to serve man. If at times nature appeared to be harmful (e.g. by producing poisonous honey), it was conveying a lesson (in this case, do not be greedy). There was, in other words, a moral dimension built in to the natural world.

Man's duty, consequently, was to respect the limits of the world and to work within them. Pliny exemplifies the problem with reference to mining. Since he too thought of earth as sacred, like a mother or nurse, he concluded that everything man needed should be available on its beneficent surface. But gold and iron had to be dug out of it, and all they did was to corrupt and harm (Pliny admits elsewhere that iron can be useful for making farm equipment, but here he is thinking of weapons). Excessive interference with nature, in other words, could only be harmful. So Pliny would not have been surprised to hear that the burning of fossil fuels dug from the earth contributed towards the 'greenhouse effect'. Of our present problems, he would argue that the earth will exact a high, and deserved, price for our insane meddling with nature.

These sorts of belief about the natural world played their part in forming Roman beliefs about its end. Lucretius, for example, argued that the world was already far past its prime and slowly exhausting itself. For all his trendy, up-to-date equipment, the farmer found it increasingly difficult to wring a living from the earth, which was now like an old woman past the age of child-bearing: 'everything is gradually decaying and nearing its end, worn out by old age.' The world would end with a whimper.

The younger Seneca, meanwhile, expressed a more apocalyptic view. Arguing that nothing is difficult for nature if she decides to destroy herself, he envisages the ending coming 'suddenly, with tremendous violence' owing to an increasing imbalance in nature, especially between land and sea. As the end draws near, winter will dominate a world where summer is no more, and even the sun and stars will fail. Finally, flood and earthquake will bury the human race in a single day in one gigantic cataclysm. The world will end with a bang.

But why? Seneca argues that the seeds of this great cataclysm were sown into the world at its birth, and that the destruction of its inhabitants is but the prelude to the creation of a new human race, ignorant of wrongdoing. But it too will not last: for 'goodness is difficult to find, and needs a director and guide, but vice is learned without any need for a teacher'. Seneca, in other words, sees a direct link between wrongdoing and survival. Noah would have approved, but 'sin' is not a concept much debated in the media today.

Natural ends

Aristotle turned respect for the workings of nature into a philosophical principle. When he wanted to explain a feature of animal or plant life, the first question he asked was 'What is its *telos*?' *Telos* meant 'end, purpose, function' and Aristotle's broad thesis was that nature did nothing in vain. So his first step was usually to try to explain what the purpose of the given feature was, on the grounds that it must have some purpose, or nature would not have permitted it. Why do ducks have webbed feet? 'So that, living in water where wings are useless, they may have feet that are useful for swimming. For they are like oars to oarsmen or fins to fish. Hence, if fish have their fins destroyed or ducks their webbing, they no longer swim.'

Not that Aristotle thinks that Nature has intentionalist designs for her creations. When he argues that 'plants produce leaves to shelter the fruit and grow roots downwards rather than upwards for the sake of nutrition', he does not thereby imagine that vegetables are capable of rational thought on the matter, or that a radish with advanced views would suddenly start growing its roots upwards. Plants and animals simply possess functional parts which demonstrate functional behaviour.

This principle has broad applications. Quite recently Home Office ministers, concerned about a nasty spate of knife attacks, wondered if it was possible to distinguish between nice and nasty knives. What is the *telos* of a bread – as opposed to a combat – knife, Aristotle would have suggested they ask, and what physical characteristics does each knife require to fulfil its *telos*? One glance at an average combat-knife, with its massive double-blade, hand-guard and puerile decorations, should have settled that argument.

VERY HUMOROUS, DOC

Western medicine has its roots in attempts by early Greek philosophers to describe how the world worked. Empedocles (fifth century BC) proposed that the four roots of all things were earth, air, fire and water. Anaxagoras (fifth century BC) argued that opposites like wet and dry, hot and cold were fundamental elements. Alcmaeon (sixth century BC) thought that health depended on a balance of conflicting forces within the body.

Observing that the body evacuated many liquids, doctors eventually settled on four (called 'humours') which they considered vital to health – blood, phlegm, yellow bile and black bile. They chose four to create a tidy match with Empedocles' four roots, Anaxagoras' four opposites and the four seasons too: so yellow bile = fire = hot = summer illnesses, etc. They assumed the body got rid of these 'humours' to maintain that balance which Alcmaeon had said good health required. This balance, they theorised, was normally maintained by the body's natural 'innate heat'. Medicine was the art of restoring that balance when nature failed.

Like all bogus dogma, this system could do everything but actually solve the problem of illness. That awaited eighteenth-century science and technology, when man could finally get below the level of what he could see with his unaided eyesight. But what one can say is that at least Greek doctors tried to be rational about it all. Given their assumptions, they attempted to build on them by logic and observation and, perhaps most important of all, demanded that anyone with a case to make about anything should give a *logos*, a 'rational account' of it, 'something that could be argued over' (see p. 37).

But that was not all. Doctors made their living by public performance. Their 'accounts', in other words, had to be both accessible to the public (democracy in action) and persuasive (see p. 42ff.). The great Greek doctor Hippocrates (fifth century BC) talks of the importance of 'making the issues intelligible to the layman'. Further, an account which one doctor might give of an illness and its likeliest cure could obviously be challenged in public debate not only by a layman but by another doctor too. Medical texts are full of combative discussions of why their way of treating patients is superior (the writer of *On Joints*, for example, registers his patients' delight at his intricate new bandaging techniques, though admits they eventually got bored with them).

Treacle down effect

One area where ancient doctors did have some success was in their medical use of plants (an area in which modern scientists too are extremely interested). The *Natural History* of Pliny the elder is full of salient information. Pliny starts with kitchen plants and first on the list is the wild cucumber. It will cure gout, toothache, impetigo, itch and deafness. Turnips, raw and mixed with salt, will deal with ailments of the foot and, like parsnips, have aphrodisiac qualities (because of their shape?). Onions are good for dog-bites and abrasions, and used as suppositories will disperse haemorrhoids. Leeks cure hangovers and impart brilliance to the voice. Garlic does almost everything, including returning madmen to sanity. Lettuce juice fixes eye-problems, checks sexual desire, and cures flatulence, belching and melancholy. And so on, for eight books.

Mithridates (120-63 BC), king of Pontus (Black Sea coast of Turkey), combined herbal and animal products (viper flesh) to discover an antidote to poison (he is said to have invented the idea of immunisation, by taking minute doses of deadly drugs – testing them on slaves first, of course). Doctors latched on to the principle to produce panaceas known as 'theriac' (Greek *thêrion*, 'wild beast'), containing hundreds of ingredients. By the fifteenth century they were often taken with molasses, which kept the various ingredients in even suspension ('treacle' derives from theriac). Theriacs were finally exposed in the eighteenth century ('never has a medicine containing so much cured so little') but are still found in the shape of 'secret' miracle cures and wonder foods.

Hippocrates' Oath

The most famous ancient doctor was Hippocrates, from the Greek island of Cos. He is best known for his Oath, now sadly abandoned by most medical schools or modernised. But that decision does not alter the importance of the Hippocratic Oath in putting democratic accountability at the heart of doctor-patient relationships.

Since there was no such thing as authorised medical training, let alone degree certificates, in the ancient world, anyone could claim to be a doctor. Before the oath was ever invented, however, the idea of the perfect doctor was already taking shape. We hear of a Greek doctor being honoured for serving 'all alike fairly, whether rich or poor, slave or free or foreigner' and that he 'maintained a blameless reputation in all respects'. Of one Xenotimos, we read that at a time of epidemic, 'of his own free will he constantly helped those who needed it; intent upon bringing recovery to all the sick indiscriminately, and toiling for all citizens equally, he saved many'.

The Hippocratic Oath, however, suggests what could go wrong. There was no point, for example, in the Oath getting the doctor to guard life and the medical art in purity and holiness, and forswear murder, euthanasia, abortifacients, sexual relationships with patients, breaking of confidentialities and general wrongdoing unless these were known to be areas where doctors could fall short. The doctor was an expert. Experts are undemocratic. Patients needed to be protected against him. This is what the Oath tried to do. This all raises the question – should today's 'expert' politicians, spin-doctors, scientists, journalists, shopkeepers, dons (etc.) also swear an Oath protecting us against them? And by what god should they swear?

Hippocrates' Oath falls into two parts. The first specifies the young doctor's duty to his teacher, his teacher's family and to any pupils he takes on. This could be made relevant to modern doctors, who are, after all, trained by the NHS and should have to make some concrete commitment to it. (Perhaps we could adopt the ancient Greek system where the trainee doctor practised on private patients before winning a proper public posting.)

In the second part of the Oath, Hippocrates reaches the heart of medical ethics. When prescribing diet, he will ensure that no one suffers harm and all are treated without fear or favour. He will neither prescribe nor even suggest drugs that could be terminal or cause abortions. He will leave surgery to the experts. When visiting homes, he will come 'dispassionately, for the benefit of the sick', and not for any other purpose (and especially not sexual relations). Finally, he will maintain strict confidentiality. All this made a great deal of sense at a time when the purpose of medicine was to deal with ill-health and deliver children safely. Nowadays, the sheer success of medicine in the west in dealing with basic health problems has created serious difficulties for it. What are its priorities now as a publicly-funded service? To keep people alive as long as possible? To force people to be healthy? To respond to anyone's 'need', whim or fantasy (women producing babies at 80 – cf. p. 15)?

'I will conduct my life and my art purely and properly' goes one part of the Oath. For Hippocrates, technical expertise, morality and love of his fellow man went hand in hand. No wonder his Oath became standard in Christian times, when even pagan doctors were hailed as 'saviours' for their altruistic philanthropy.

Bedside manners

Greek doctors fully understood the psychology of medicine and the importance of keeping the patient happy, and ancient Greek medical writings are full of advice to doctors on how to behave. One treatise, for example, commands a doctor to 'appear healthy and plump, otherwise he will not be thought capable of looking after even himself'. He must be clean, well-dressed and sweet-smelling. Another treatise urges doctors to watch out for patients' misbehaviour: 'they often lie about taking the medicine you have prescribed. They won't take any they don't like, never admit it, and the doctor gets the blame if they die.' This treatise goes on to suggest the doctor should 'not say too much about present and future condition, since this often causes a setback'.

But the most sensitive issue of all was sexual. Since Greek males believed that women were sexually irresistible and entirely lacking in self-control, any alien male in the house posed a serious threat, let alone a doctor. One treatise advises: 'there is close intimacy between patient and doctor and patients put themselves entirely under his control. Since he is meeting women, virgins and most precious possessions at every turn, he must maintain rigorous self-control in all respects.' That is why the Hippocratic Oath contained the clause: 'I will not abuse my position to indulge in sexual contacts with the bodies of women or men, whether they be freemen or slaves.'

The purpose of this accountability was to maintain the doctor's personal status and inspire confidence and trust in the patient, in order to get repeat business. The writer of the treatise *Precepts* puts it on a higher level: 'he who loves mankind also loves medicine.' Commitment to medicine is the same as commitment to humanity.

Fit, not fat

Ancient doctors would probably have approved of today's government bleating away about the evils of smoking, drinking and so on. It would have brought them business. They were well aware, for example, of the dangers of one favourite modern problem condition, obesity. Hippocrates knew that sudden death was more common in the fat. Both he and Aristotle thought that fatness in women caused sterility – a sufficient reason for the ancients to condemn female obesity – but we do not hear of anorexia or anyone slimming for aesthetic reasons. Hippocrates got close, suggesting that a large physique was pleasing in the young, though not in the old, but recommended moderation in dieting: 'dieting which causes excessive loss of weight, as well as the feeding-up of the emaciated, is beset with difficulties.'

In Greek eyes, obesity was particularly associated with luxury. Ptolemy Alexander I (*c.* 140-88 BC), a Greek king of Egypt, needed two people to support him when he left the room to relieve himself. The vast Dionysius, tyrant of Heracleia on the south coast of the Black Sea from 337-305 BC, in danger of choking if he fell deeply asleep, had to be pricked awake with very fine needles long enough to locate the nerves under the rolls of flesh. Yet he lived to fifty-five, tyrant for thirty-three years, 'excelling all in gentleness and decency'. On their tomb-paintings, seventh-century BC Etruscans (north of Rome) tended to depict aristocrats at dinner as very fat and even more contented. Spartans took a stern government line: their warriors were inspected naked every ten days for signs of excessive thinness or corpulence.

But what action to take? The Roman doctor Celsus (first century AD) recommended thin men put on weight through rest, constipation and big meals, and that the fat take it off through late nights, worry and violent exercise. Can't argue with that, doc.

Street medicine

But what about the cost of modern medicine? As Health Secretaries seek ever more efficient ways of ensuring that no treatment is ever available to anyone on the NHS (one remembers intriguing plans for 'hospitals without walls'), they may as well adopt the completely doctorless scheme of medical care reported by Herodotus.

On his journeys to Babylonia (modern Iraq), Herodotus was surprised to observe that, unlike Greeks, the Babylonians had no doctors, but that anyone who fell ill was immediately taken on to the street and left there. The point was that no passer-by was allowed to walk past the ill in silence. Custom demanded that they had to ask what the trouble was. The invalid then had to explain, and after that it was the responsibility of the passer-by to offer the sufferer advice on his complaint. The passer-by could speak from personal experience, or from his observations of similar complaints in others, and Herodotus observed that 'anyone will stop by the sick man's side and suggest remedies which he has himself proved successful in whatever the trouble may be, or which he has known to succeed with other people'.

Herodotus lived in a world well-peopled with doctors whose highest ambition was to serve the public. Nevertheless, he was greatly taken by the ingenuity of this 'Neighbourhood Nostrum' scheme. Since everyone who is sick loves to talk about it, as does everyone who has been dramatically cured, it is an efficient way of pooling common experience. It would save the NHS billions a year in the tiresome business of looking after the ill which so interrupts the really important work of filling in forms. And no system could be more consumer-driven.

THINK SHRINK

Psychotherapy (ancient Greek: 'psyche-care') seems to be all the rage at the moment. The help seems to consist not of practical advice but of a soothing, mantric vocabulary, endlessly repeated – 'the need for personal space', 'finding myself', 'a cry for help', 'self-assertion', 'nurturance' and so on (cf. p. 9).

Plato took a different view. For him, problems were solved by thinking straight. For that to happen, the *psyche* (Greek *psukhê*) must be ruled by reason. Plato's *psyche* (meaning roughly 'mind'/ 'soul'/ 'self') consisted of three parts – the 'rational' part (concerned with timeless truth and ultimate reality), the 'irrational' (concerned with the appetites), and the 'spirited' (which formed emotional responses and gave the energy to the other parts to pursue what they desired). For a person to be happy, the rational part, with its commitment to absolute truth, needed cultivation. Fearing that the irrational part, lusting for bodily pleasures, would overwhelm the other two, Plato proposed a two-stage educational programme to forge consensus between the three parts, so that they would agree together and live in harmony under reason's rule. It was a programme in which pupils were led by the example of, and discussion with, reason-ruled people to distinguish between right and wrong action and thought.

Aristotle was interested not so much in happiness as in success. Success was 'an activity of the *psyche* in accordance with excellence', and by 'excellence' he meant excellence in that which differentiated us from animals and made us human – reason and thought. Success, then, required that a man become engaged in intellectual activity. Further, he went on, goodness depended on making (reasoned) choices, and since choice was 'deliberate desire, the reasoning must be true and the desire right'. He too saw that reason and desire could work in harmony.

Modern psychotherapy offers the client a cosy language designed, it seems, to justify the client's behaviour. Whether the problem then goes away is a nice question, but at least the client feels better. Ancient Greeks would have regarded that as a cop-out. True care of the *psyche* for them required more than forms of words – it required disciplined action. Nowadays a more Platonic approach is gaining ground. Psychoanalysis, invented by Freud in 1896 to cure psychopathic disorders by investigation of the 'unconscious mind', is being challenged by 'cognitive therapy', whose aim is to get sufferers to think properly about their problems. All this is a far cry from the expensive mysteries of the psychiatrist's couch and Freud's assertion that the difference between the unconscious and conscious mind matters, let alone that the unconscious is more important. Time for reason to return to its throne.

Memory man

Plato is a true Greek in his belief in the power of the mind. Greek literature, from Homer onwards, often presented behaviour as the product not of deep, unknowable psychological forces but of intellectual choice (but see p. 1). A wild fighter in Homer is described as 'knowing wildness'. 'Know yourself' was a piece of popular wisdom: know what you can and what you *cannot* do, and you will get by.

Socrates took this tendency to its logical extreme when he developed his famous paradox 'no one goes/does wrong intentionally'. Socrates believed that true happiness depended on knowledge – knowledge, that is, of goodness. If one knew what was good, one would do it, because the result was guaranteed to be happiness (hence 'goodness is knowledge'). To the objection that people often know what is good but still do not do it, Socrates argued that they cannot in that case *really* know it: their judgement is clouded.

Plato's radical insistence on the importance of using your conscious mind to make decisions (radical by today's standards, at any rate) does, however, come up against something of a philosophical brick wall. If you are looking for e.g. goodness because you do not know what it is, how do you know it when you have found it? Plato's answer was that you do indeed know what you are looking for: for knowledge is recollection (*anamnêsis*). All of us, he argued, are immortal souls: when we die, our soul transmigrates into a different body (animal or human) and, in a thousand years, returns to earth. So we know things in this life because we can recollect things we learnt from previous lives, whether on earth or in Hades. Indeed, we in fact know *everything*, if only we could recollect it.

Plato 'proves' this theory by a famous experiment with a slave. Guided by Socrates with some pretty leading questions, the slave is shown to know Pythagoras' theorem. But he has never learnt even maths, let alone the theorem. How then can he know it? Answer: by recollection (*anamnêsis*) of a previous existence, when he *did* know it. Q.E.D.

It is a great relief that Plato is not on the reading list of those unscrupulous American psychologists who have been using 'memory recovery' to 'prove' to the suggestible that their parents abused them when they were young. If he was, they could encourage the suggestible to recollect abuse not only from this life, but from previous lives too. Then they could track down *those* abusers (whose souls must be somewhere) and destroy them and *their* families as well.

3

Laws, Rights and Wrongs

The rafts of legislation pouring out of government and Brussels would have struck the Greek philosopher Plato as profoundly disturbing.

In his *Republic* (c. 375 BC), Plato argues that the key to a healthy society is a proper education – the 'one big thing' as Plato calls it, from which everything else follows (cf. p. 121ff.). Get that right, and 'the process of growth will be cumulative. A good education system produces people of good character; and they in turn produce children better than themselves, and so it goes on. Animals provide a good analogy.'

Once the young are educated not in rules but principles, proper behaviour like 'being silent in the presence of elders, giving up your seat to them, standing when they enter the room, and looking after your parents' is automatic, and issues of 'hairstyle, clothing, footwear and the general way one presents oneself' solve themselves. Significantly, he goes on: 'In my opinion only an idiot would legislate on such matters. These rules do not come into being, nor would they remain in force, through being formulated and written down.'

The result will be that people see what is right and wrong without prompting. The same, argues Plato, goes for the world of business. 'Contracts with labourers, lawsuits, empanelling juries, rent-collection, regulations affecting markets, or police, or ports – shall we take on legislation and rules in these matters?' Of course not, he goes on. Properly educated people will work this all out for themselves – as long as the principles of their education are sound.

If, however, their education is valueless, 'they will spend their whole time making and correcting detailed regulations, in the hope that they'll achieve perfection. They'll live like the ill, who lack the discipline to give up a way of life that is bad for them. All their treatments get them nowhere, yet they live in hope that their next recommended medicine will restore them to health, and detest those who suggest that, until they put an end to their lifestyle, no amount of medicine or cautery or surgery will do them any good at all.' He concludes that it is the mark of a badly governed society to need rafts of legislation about everything. Such law-makers, he goes on in a brilliant image, 'are unaware of the fact that they are like people who are slashing away at a kind of Hydra' – the many-headed monster which grew two heads for every one chopped off.

The well-governed citizens of the Greek community of Locris, so the Greek orator Demosthenes (fourth century BC) tells us, were firmly convinced that their forefathers had got everything right and followed Plato to the letter. They refused to allow anyone to propose a new law without first placing a rope round his neck. If the proposal was rejected, the noose was pulled tight and he was dead.

They had a law which ordered any man who had put out another man's eye to be punished by having his own eye put out (there was no alternative of a fine). There then came along a man (Demosthenes continues) with one eye, and an enemy of his (who had two eyes) threatened to put it out. Reflecting that life would not be worth living if he lost his one remaining eye, and on the principle that he had nothing to lose anyway, the man put his neck in the noose and proposed that anyone who put out the eye of a man who had just one should himself lose both, so that their sufferings would be similar. The proposal was accepted – the only new law, Demosthenes tells us, passed in Locris for some two hundred years.

The Locrians' method of curbing legislation looks as good as any, though the rush of people to pull the rope would take some controlling. Perhaps it could feature as top prize in the Lottery one week? Interestingly, an American judge recently ordered a young man who put out another man's eye to serve part of his prison sentence wearing an eye-patch, so that he could get some sense of what his victim had to suffer. Not so novel, judge.

Courting trouble

Ancient Greeks were as keen as we are to resolve disputes early and prevent them coming to court. In Athens, the aggrieved party first gathered witnesses and confronted his opponent with his claim. That might settle the matter on the spot. If not, the parties then had the option of going to *private* arbitration. They agreed on the arbitrators and their terms of reference, and contracted to stand by the decision, which had judicial force.

If they could not agree to this, a summons was served orally, and the

An eye for an eye

two parties were told to appear with witnesses on the stated day before the *arkhon* (a public legal official). The *arkhon's* job was to decide whether the case was actionable, this time by *public* arbitration. If it was, the plaint was formally deposed in writing while the accused could also lodge an official objection. Both sides put down a cash sum against costs (the loser of the case paid up), and the plaint was displayed in public.

On the day of the hearing, both sides swore an oath that they were telling the truth and presented their evidence before the public arbitrator (not an official, but an Athenian citizen beyond military age selected by lot). If a decision was reached, the matter ended there. If not, it went to the full court (see p. 73). The evidence, which could not now be added to, was sealed up in a box (*ekhinos*, literally 'hedgehog' or 'sea-urchin') to be read out in court when the time came. At any time, the parties could agree to revert to private arbitration.

Take the case of Neaera (fourth century BC). She was a (non-Athenian) slave, and had been saving up to buy her freedom. When the Athenian Phrynion donated a large sum to help her, she gratefully went to live with him in Athens. But he started taking her round to high-class orgies and after a while she decided she had had enough. She took what she reckoned she was entitled to, and walked out. After various adventures, she re-settled in Athens with one Stephanus. When Phrynion heard of this, he stormed round to Stephanus' place: she was his and he wanted her and his property back. Stephanus countered that Neaera had bought her freedom and could co-habit with whomever she pleased.

The case went to arbitration. The sides appointed one mediator each, and agreed a third. They decided that Neaera was a free woman; she should give back to Phrynion everything except the clothes, jewels and personal maids; and she should live with and be maintained by each man on alternate days (unless they agreed some other system).

Cutting costs

Greek ways of doing things would help solve the problem of e.g. strikes and excessive awards in libel and other cases that so bedevil our system today. In 399 BC Socrates was charged with not believing in the old gods, introducing new gods, and corrupting the youth of Athens – the occasion in memory of which Plato constructed his famous *Apology* (literally 'defence speech') of Socrates. The trial took the usual form: the prosecution speech (by Meletus) was followed with the defence speech (by Socrates) before a jury of 501 randomly-selected

Athenian (male) citizens over 30, who without further discussion voted on the issue.

Socrates was found guilty as charged, though the vote was close (221-280). But since no penalty was prescribed by law, it fell to both parties to *propose* a penalty and invite the jury to decide. The prosecution demanded the death penalty. Socrates, typically, argued that, since his life had been beneficial to Athens, he should not be punished but rewarded. The state should therefore maintain him for the rest of his life. His friends, appalled by his suggestion, quickly clubbed together to propose a fine. Socrates grudgingly agreed. The jury voted for the death penalty.

This is the way ahead for e.g. libel cases. After a guilty verdict, let defence and prosecution counsels both propose damages, and the jury decide. Neither side will risk extremes in case they alienate the jury (Socrates' downfall?). Sense will then prevail. Strikes should be handled in the same way. Forget those all-night discussions to 'thrash out' a compromise 'round the table', with 'negotiators' engaging in 'shuttle diplomacy' trying to 'break the deadlock' between the two parties. In cases where the national interest is at stake, let both sides table their proposals and the people vote on them.

BY RIGHTS

A teacher at a Catholic school, Shairon Rodgers (and she certainly did), had three children by three different fathers (an ex-husband, a fellow teacher, and a former pupil). She was astonished to be asked by the governors to leave. 'I have a right to a personal life and a right to have a baby', she protested. Ancient Greeks would have found incomprehensible this appeal to 'rights', now routinely intoned by anybody who thinks they have been hard done by. The reason is that Greeks did not regard the state as the means by which individual freedoms were to be protected.

A concept such as 'conscientious objection', for example, would have seemed to them absurd. At one time Socrates found himself chairman of a powerful public committee which had a tricky question to decide – should those admirals who had failed to pick up the survivors after the battle of Arginusae (406 BC) be tried *en bloc* or not? Trial *en bloc* was illegal, but the Assembly cried for a vote in favour to be taken on the matter, and the committee became so terrified they agreed – all except Socrates. His reasoning, reported by soldier-historian Xenophon, was nothing to do with conscientious objection – 'Socrates said that he would act only in accordance with the law'.

This is the nub. On the question of rights, Greeks would have asked only 'What does the law say?' For Mrs Rodgers, then, to claim a 'right' to a personal life or a baby would have appeared well-nigh meaningless: as well claim a 'right' to cough. The point is that an appeal to 'rights' these days is a device designed to end argument. It just sounds better than a 'demand'. It invites no further discussion.

On the real issue – the question of the relationship between Mrs Rodgers' 'right' to a sex-life and her job – Greeks would have acted like those provident school governors and asked 'Do we want a person like Mrs Rodgers teaching impressionable youth at a school like ours, whatever her "rights"?'

Private passions

A more interesting modern case involved the men imprisoned in the recent 'Spanner' trial for engaging voluntarily in sado-masochistic activities. The 'Spanner' defence rested on two principles: the right to privacy, and the famous equity maxim *volenti non fit injuria* 'no harm is done to a willing participant'. The court found that consent does not turn an illegal act into a legal one.

Ancient Greeks would also have rejected both principles. First, as we have seen, Greeks never talked about 'rights', only about laws (the concept of 'rights' is comparatively recent – Bill of Rights 1689, Rousseau's Social Contract 1762, the American Constitution 1791, The Universal Declaration of Human Rights 1948 – and 'rights' to what seems anti-social behaviour does not seem a helpful concept). Second, Greeks thought primarily in terms of the community's, not the individual's, good. So the issues of 'privacy' and 'willingness' would have been irrelevant too. As a result, Greek arguments would have centred on public interest: e.g. did this sort of thing weaken military capacity, corrupt the young? (etc.). This to us is totalitarian. It represents a frame of mind we slip into, perhaps, only in war.

Incidentally, Greeks and Romans did not seem to engage in serious sado-masochism for sexual purposes. The closest one gets is the use of the slipper in erotic scenes painted on vases. But they were fascinated by what makes humans behave as they do. Epicurus, for example, classified 'desire' into three categories: (i) natural and necessary, (ii) natural and unnecessary, and (iii) unnatural and unnecessary, and argued that the first guaranteed a trouble-free life. The 'Spanner' defendants would surely have struck Epicurus as exemplifying in extreme form the third, least desirable category.

The relationship between private but offensive (usually sexual) behaviour, people's reaction to it and the law has always been tricky. Pericles' idealisation of Athens in his famous Funeral Speech (430 BC) comes to mind: 'Far from spying jealously on each other, we do not feel called upon to be angry with our neighbour for doing what he likes, or even to indulge in those hard looks which are offensive, though inflicting no positive penalty. But this ease in our private relations does not make us lawless as citizens.'

BASIC INSTINCTS

Athenians did legislate about some sexual conduct. An offended husband could kill an adulterer on the spot; sexual acts against free (not slave) minors were punished outright. But the law did not try to root out immorality; rather, it indicated where the limits of state intrusion into private life should be drawn. For example, a male who allowed himself to be used 'like a woman' was banned from political life. Politics was man's business in ancient Athens: behaviour so perverted would surely taint public life. So the state felt it right in this case to intervene.

In so legislating, Greeks put a very high priority on the privacy of the home. Intrusions here, it was felt, really did threaten public order. Thus while the male adulterer was punishable by law because he was an outsider who threatened its very basis, the woman was not (she was merely divorced). On the same principle, rape seems to have been less of an offence than seduction, because it did not alienate the woman's affection and so threaten the very heart of the family.

Outside the law, as the politician Demosthenes argued, 'a man can do and say whatever he likes as long as he does not care what reputation such conduct brings him'. That is very Greek – reputation in the public eye is all (see p. 103). So status-mad Greeks would have been baffled, for example, by the way leading politicians have affairs with dreary assortments of bimbos and secretaries. How can that improve their status? If a Greek had been the slightest bit interested in a politician's sexual life rather than in his political performance, he might perhaps have proposed a motion forcing politicians today to list mistresses as well as business connections. At least they might then contemplate affairs with someone interesting. Again, if they must have affairs, why do they not have them in the nation's interest? Like Julius Caesar with Cleopatra and Alexander with Roxana, they could do tremendous good by cosying up to the lovely Mrs Arafat, say, or exotic Mrs Hussein.

Marital lex

Romans did try moral legislation from time to time. The first Roman emperor Augustus became very worried about the decline in both moral standards and birth-rate among the upper-classes. If Rome was to be great again, it must regenerate the past, he thought. So in 18 BC, the notorious old adulterer launched a back-to-basics campaign, to stamp on adultery and force the upper-classes to marry and have children.

First, adultery became a public crime as well as a private offence. A wronged husband could prosecute both wife and lover, with punishments including even exile. Then a marriage-law was passed which placed liabilities on those who did not marry (men between twenty-five and sixty, women between twenty and fifty); and further liabilities if they did not have any children. The first liability was that the property of the childless automatically reverted to the state; the second that, because there were strict age-limits to the holding of key offices in Rome, the number of a man's children gave him precedence when he put himself up for office (the more children he had, the earlier he could stand). Obey the law, in other words, and watch the advantages accrue.

The Romans deeply resented the whole fatuous scheme and it did not last. But Romans did interfere where society had a legitimate interest – in the raising of children (cf. p. 8).

Child protection

The two most ancient ceremonial forms of Roman marriage transferred the wife and all her property into the full control of her husband, but these gradually went out of favour and were replaced by a third form – *usus* ('usage'). This was a matter of a simple union between two Roman citizens. Man and woman lived together for a year to become officially married (no formalities of any sort were required), and the wife remained wholly free of her husband's control if she spent three nights a year away from him. A wife married by *usus* also kept control over all her property (unlike women married by the formal methods), and it was forbidden for one partner to make donations (beyond basic upkeep) to the other. To divorce they simply separated. Nothing more was required. Consequently, there was no legal or religious compulsion to stay together, no traumatic (and expensive) divorce cases, and no arguments over financial settlements. As for children, again there was no argument. Whatever the circumstances, they belonged to the father.

Would it work in today's world? One might argue that a woman would think twice about having children unless she had absolute confidence in the stability of their marriage; and that no man with an eye on pastures new would want to be encumbered (by law) with children from an old relationship. The Roman way might concentrate the mind of both partners precisely where society's interests really are at stake – the secure rearing of children (cf. p. 8).

SOFT OPTION

Every Home Secretary huffs and puffs and promises 'to get tough with criminals'. This is very Roman. The Greek philosopher Plato, on the other hand, might well have urged him to get soft.

Prevention was not a marked feature of the Roman punishment system. Jailing was rare in antiquity, though the more common forced labour had the same effect, and though correction was discussed ('severity is the best corrective, but if overdone loses its effectiveness' – Seneca) it does not seem to have had any effect upon attitudes to punishment. Deterrence was better understood. A Roman lawyer comments that criminals are hung on gallows in places they frequented in order to deter others and comfort the relatives of their victims; and Romans on occasions punished criminals in gruesome public 'charades' in which the malefactors were dressed up as mythical characters and appropriately despatched (e.g. being burned to death in the guise of Hercules, who died on a pyre). But for the most part Romans punished people for the purpose of retribution and revenge: the criminal should suffer in turn something of the suffering he had caused. Hard labour was supposed to be just that, and in the case of the death penalty the worst offenders had to suffer horribly in the process of dying. It was also important to humiliate the criminal – e.g. the soldiers' mockery of Jesus – and some crimes had different punishments related to the offender's class.

Plato, however, was one of the few ancients to take seriously the idea that the purpose of punishment was to reform the criminal – by any means at all. To that extent, the recent system of 'camps' for juvenile offenders that seem to turn into something more like holiday camps might have appealed to him.

The Greek law-giver Solon (sixth century BC) argued that a community was held together by rewards and penalties, and the earliest Greek law-codes back him up, prescribing punishments on a wide scale. The general aim seems to have been to get some compensation for crimes committed. This acted as a deterrent, while satisfying affronted feelings and showing who was boss. But there were other reactions. The orator Isocrates discussed the social causes of crime, and advocated prevention rather than punishment. The thinker Protagoras favoured penalties, but rather to help the reform of the criminal than to reflect the severity of the crime. Plato went the whole hog. For him, crime was a moral error, a disease, and needed to be cured.

This did not mean that the criminal could get away without paying compensation or being punished. Far from it. But the purpose of the punishment should be to cure the disease which had caused the criminal to act as he did in the first place. Consequently, punishment could take any number of forms. As Plato says in his *Laws*, 'we may take action against the criminal, or simply talk to him; we may grant him pleasures or make him suffer; we may honour him or disgrace him, fine him or give him gifts. We may use absolutely any means to make him hate injustice and embrace true justice – or at any rate, not hate it.' So Plato would have been perfectly happy with adventure holidays, expensive cruises and relaxing boot-camps for criminals, on one condition only – that they cured the disease. But cured the disease must be.

Punishing pleasures

In his dialogue *Gorgias* Plato (through the mouth of Socrates) follows up his theory of punishment with an astonishing claim – that the criminal who has been punished for his crimes with rack, torture or even death is happier than the criminal who has not. The argument goes like this. Crime deserves punishment; therefore punishment is just. Justice is the greatest good; therefore the punished criminal is experiencing the greatest good, while the unpunished is not. Goodness results in happiness; therefore the punished criminal is happier than the unpunished. This argument fits neatly into a wider Platonic theory, that committing a crime is like falling ill. Are you ill? Go to your doctor and get better. Have you committed a crime? Go to your punisher and get better.

Socrates is unrelenting in his application of this theory. It is a man's duty, he says, to denounce himself, his family and friends if they commit any crimes, because punishment is in their best interests, the only way to restore them to health and happiness. Likewise, if you want to be really nasty to your enemy, encourage him in wickedness, for that will certainly lead to his ultimate damnation. Incidentally, Plato argues in his *Laws* that those who commit suicide to escape punishment are guilty of such 'slothful and abject cowardice' that they should be buried in disgrace in an unmarked, single grave, far away in a lonely, unnamed spot.

Capital threat

Ancients were not sensitive about killing people. This sensitivity seems to be a peculiarly twentieth-century phenomenon, reasons for which are worth, but do not receive, debate. So ancients would have found the unquestioned concept of the 'sanctity of human life' bewildering. In Rome, for example, a huge range of offences was subject to capital punishment (e.g. everything at various times from predicting the future of the imperial house to tampering with gold coins). Greeks debated capital punishment in terms of their self-interest. In 427 BC Athens put down the revolt of the city of Mytilene on the island of Lesbos. The Athenian Assembly angrily voted to execute all adult males and sell the women and children into slavery, and a ship was sent to see to it. But next day the debate was re-opened, as the fifth-century BC Athenian historian Thucydides tells us, because 'people began to think how cruel and unprecedented it was to destroy everyone, not just the guilty'.

Thucydides polarises the debate round two speeches, both of which avoid issues of pity, fairness and justice and concentrate on self-interest. Cleon argues that the people must not become 'guilty of weakness which is dangerous to you and will not make [your enemies] love you any more ... you will not make them obey you by injuring your own interests to do them a favour ... it is fatal to pass measures and not abide by them ... humans despise those who treat them well, but look up to those who make no concessions'.

Diodotus warns against decisions made in haste and anger. Capital punishment never deterred anyone intent on trouble: it will only make other cities plan their revolts more thoroughly. To execute the innocent will alienate those who never opposed Athens in the first place, and will ensure full turn-outs for future revolts since Athens treats innocent and guilty alike. The best long-term security is so to treat others that they will not want to revolt. That is where Athenian self-interest lies in this case.

Diodotus' motion won by a whisker. A ship was despatched at full speed to catch the one sent out earlier, and reached Mytilene just in time to stop wholesale massacre. Good principle, self-interest. But it is interesting that parliament is forbidden by EU legislation even to discuss capital punishment. There is something very odd going on here. Where, for example, members of a community intentionally set out to destroy that community, no Greek or Roman would think twice about doing away with them.

The most famous subject of capital punishment in the Greek world was Socrates. We are not told how long he took to die in the state prison in Athens in 399 BC, but as Plato describes it in his dialogue *Phaedo*, it was an easy death. Socrates drank up his hemlock, walked around and lay down when his legs felt heavy. He lost all sensation in his feet and legs; the numbness spread to his waist; and when it reached his heart, he twitched once and died. Almost to the last he chatted with his friends, and even cracked a joke about the god of healing.

The truth is likely to have been rather different. In his *Antidotes to Poison*, Nicander (second century BC) describes the numbness in the legs that Plato records, but adds 'the eyes roll, victims totter round the streets and crawl on their hands; their lower throat and windpipe is blocked and chokes, their arteries contract ... they draw breath like one swooning'. Modern accounts add nausea, vomiting, salivation and convulsions (Socrates' last twitch?).

Plato was being selective in the picture he drew of Socrates' end. He wanted to remove any indignity from his revered teacher's last moments and to portray Socrates as master over his body even in death. Perhaps too, as Socrates slowly lost sensation, Plato imagined his soul slowly freeing itself from the body's prison into that afterlife they had just been discussing.

4

Politics and Corruption, Europe and the Lords

The Labour leader Tony Blair has proudly announced that we are a 'stakeholder society' and should all have stakes in things. What things, however, remain to be seen. Certainly no one is going to be allowed to have a stake in parliament. The ancient Greeks were the only people ever to have had a serious stake in that, for one simple reason – there was no parliament. The Greek man in the street held all the power, and that is the true meaning of demo-cracy – 'people-power'. The invention of democracy in 507 BC was the work of the Athenian Cleisthenes – a deeply radical experiment in government, never repeated in the history of the world after it was ended by diktat of the Macedonian super-power in 322 BC.

In fifth-century BC Athens, all Athenian-born males over eighteen, irrespective of wealth or status, had the right to attend the Assembly (*ecclêsia*). This met roughly every nine days. There they discussed and decided how Athens should be run. So the people decided, for example, to declare war (or peace), levy taxes, repair the shipyards, build the Parthenon, put X into a position of power, or remove Y from his.

But thousands of Athenians could not just turn up and talk, as if from a blank sheet. An agenda for the day needed to be prepared and this was done by the Council (*boulê*), which consisted of five hundred Athenian males over thirty, drawn *by lot* from the ten 'tribes' (fifty from each tribe). Each Councillor served for one year only, and could never serve for more than two. One of the Council's main functions was to receive business, discuss it, determine if it needed action, and if it did, put it in the shape of a motion for the Assembly to debate. At any one time, fifty Council members were on 24-hour standby duty (and called the *prutaneis* in this role) to receive business, call emergency meetings, and so on (see p. 115).

The motions put by the Council to the Assembly could take one of two formats: either a precise form of words ('the Assembly should decree that ...'), or a question ('The Assembly should discuss what to do about ...'). But in all cases, it was the controlling principle of Athenian democracy that the Assembly was sovereign. If the Assembly did not like what the Council had proposed, it could throw it out, amend it, put forward an entirely different version or ask the Council to do so. At all events, once a decision was taken by the Assembly, it was up to the Council to ensure it was put into effect.

But there was more to democracy than deciding state policy. Every executive post (i.e. those people appointed to put the Assembly's will into action, rather like today's civil servants) was open to anyone who applied for it, and the final choice made mostly by *lot*. As Aristotle saw, elections are an aristocratic procedure because they are designed to choose the best. Only lottery is truly democratic. Such posts, of unrepeatable one-year tenure, dealt with such matters as temple-repairs, city works, markets, weights and measures, law-courts, public decrees, public audits, road-building, and so on.

Finally, the legal system. Here again, the law was in the hands of the citizen body, meeting either in Assembly (for certain types of procedures) or in randomly appointed courts of law, with freedom (within the law) to reach whatever decision they liked about anything. There were no judges, law-lords, barristers, solicitors or rules of precedent: just several hundred (the number varied) males over thirty, listening to one prosecution and one defence speech, and (without further discussion) voting.

Modern demockery

Now compare our system. We elect about 650 MPs to take political decisions for five years without further reference to us. Those decisions are executed by appointed, not elected, civil servants, with jobs for life. The law is the exclusive domain of appointed, not elected, judges. Whatever this is, it is most definitely not 'democracy' in the original meaning of the word.

So when newspapers and organisations like Charter 88 start sounding off ever more pompously about Democracy and Reform and The People's Chance To Make Their Voices Heard, and Lord Jenkins drones on about the importance of his proposals to 'increase democracy by proportional representation', it is as well to remind ourselves that all talk about democratic involvement is in fact so much drivel. We do not live in a democracy. We are not involved. We are very firmly excluded.

At this point it is traditional for people to object that Athens was not 'really' a democracy because women and slaves did not get the vote, and the system was 'built on slavery'. But when did even all males (over 21) get the vote in the UK? 1918. And all women on the same terms as men? 1928. As for slaves, it is difficult to remember exactly when we gave *them* the vote, but we certainly did not end slavery in the British empire till 1833, so every British achievement up till then was 'built on slavery'. Hang your heads in *shame*, Newton, Cromwell, Shakespeare and Elizabeth I. Given that abysmal record, why single out the Athenians for opprobrium? What was unique about their achievement was that all male citizens meeting in Assembly determined all public policy and any male citizen could hold executive office by simple virtue of his citizenship. We have had that example before us for 2,500 years and done nothing about it.

'Ah, but we live in a *representative* democracy' is the next objection. But representative of whom? The parties do not represent *us*: they represent themselves. When did the British people last determine a policy? Parties choose the election candidates and policies and then run parliament their own sweet way, only during elections sucking up to us as if *we* had made the policies they impose on us. Indeed, not even parliament is democratic. MPs vote as they are told, or else. That is why, if you whisper the word 'referendum' in the ear of virtually any MP, they will react as if poked with a cattle prod. The people cannot be allowed to decide things, surely. That's not democratic.

We live, in other words, in an elective oligarchy – rule by a few (oligarchs) who are elected every five years. Why not admit it? There is nothing wrong with it, after all. As Herodotus says in a famous debate, oligarchy is a matter of 'choosing a certain number of the best men in the country and giving them power ... it is natural to suppose the best men will produce the best policy'. Jolly sensible. Some day, of course, we might give democracy a whirl. Meanwhile, let us rejoice in western oligarchy and not pretend it is anything else. Aristotle, who favoured 'middle ways' would, I suspect, have rather approved of it. Meanwhile it would relieve us all of a great deal of tedious hypocrisy if politicians who magnanimously promise 'stakes' in any number of other people's businesses, but never in the only one that really counts, their own power to rule, would quietly shut up. Greeks would have found it wonderfully ironical that the 'mother of parliaments' and 'home of democracy' has a notice outside it saying 'no admittance to the general public'. That just about sums up British and western 'democracy'.

In fact, since in our system it is obvious that MPs are not experts (observe how they move from Health one day to Education the next and the Treasury the next), there is a case for saying that they should be appointed by lot, with limited, unrepeatable, tenure of office, from citizens putting themselves forward. Thus we could at last bid farewell to the pointlessly competing parties. It is the top civil servants who are the real experts. They are the ones who should be appointed by election.

Control Greeks

Greeks were not stupid. They were well aware of the contradictions and dangers in their policy of appointing people to executive office by lot. So positions demanding real expertise, i.e. top naval, military and treasury officers, were elected, and the people appointed to these posts could be re-elected (no one-year rule here). Then again, before taking up office, officials underwent a scrutiny (*dokimasia*) by a jury of the people, and had to show that they had (i) been Athenian citizens for three generations, (ii) treated their parents with proper respect, (iii) looked after their family tomb, (iv) fulfilled their military obligations, (v) paid their taxes and (vi) adopted certain state cults. Note the especial emphasis on care for the family, and then fulfilment of certain state and religious duties (p. 32).

Very few candidates indeed seem to have been rejected at the *dokimasia*. The point is that practical Greeks, once satisfied of a person's general character, were really interested only in whether they could do the job – and the one sure way of finding out was to let them get on with it.

But what if they were a failure? This is where the sanctions bite. In Athens, officials were subject to a *second* audit, at the *end* of their office, and it was now that incompetence and failure were punished. So the main check on citizens applying for office in the first place was the rigour with which they knew the Assembly examined the record of those who served them as executives, and the ferocity with which they punished anyone who let them down. Fines, loss of rights, exile, even the death penalty were all available. Indeed, politician Demosthenes said of the top ten military officials that they were more likely to die at the hands of the state executioner than in the battle line, and the figures we have suggest he was right.

So Athenians would have been astonished that our MPs and civil servants could not be punished for wrong decisions, unless being sent to the House of Lords is punishment. They would have been appalled at the infamous law lords' ruling that a minister (the wretched Kenneth Baker, in 1991) could be guilty of contempt of court, but since he was guilty 'only in an official capacity', no punitive action was appropriate. In what *other* capacity does a minister need to be guilty, for heaven's sake?

But it was not just officials who stood in the firing-line. In Athens, the people in Assembly reserved the right to impeach, retrospectively if necessary, *anyone* (official or not) who was considered to have harmed their interests (see p. 105). Thus any private citizen who had proposed a motion in the Assembly which was agreed but turned out to be a disaster could be accused of having 'proposed an illegal decree', despite the fact that the Assembly had accepted it at the time. No nonsense about 'parliamentary privilege' in Athens. Athenians, then, would have regarded it as laughable to impeach President Clinton over private, sexual conduct. Athenians impeached on what counted – *policies*. Would that we did.

Pulling power

But all this raises the obvious question – how did the whole process work? Did the people not keep changing their minds? How could such a system generate consistent policy? What role was played by individuals such as, for example, Pericles? The answer is very simple. People like Pericles, an aristocrat who was elected by the people to one of the top ten military executive positions almost every year from 443 till his death in 429 BC, wielded no constitutional power of any sort at all. They wielded authority only in as far as they could *persuade* the Assembly that they were right (see p. 42ff.). Naturally, when Pericles spoke, the Assembly listened hard because they had come to trust him: indeed, so influential did he become that the historian Thucydides said of that period that Athens was nominally a democracy but in fact was ruled by one man. If that is a correct assessment, however, that 'rule' was by virtue of the power of Pericles' oratory alone and his understanding of where his power lay – in the Assembly, and especially among the rowers of the famous Greek trireme, which raced up and down the Thames so movingly in 1993 to celebrate the 2,500th anniversary of Greek democracy outside the home of oligarchy.

The trireme played a major part in the development of Athenian democracy. These Athenian war-ships were rowed not by slaves (though they could be if needed), nor by aristocrats, but largely by free, poor Athenian citizens (with mercenary help) who were paid for the privilege. The wealth and power of Athens, which ruled the seas and kept its empire together with its fleet, depended entirely on them. Knowing well how much the empire depended on them, the rowers were a united body. So, with a navy made up of 200 such triremes, the voting power of the oarsmen at the Assembly was immense. Aristocratic statesmen like Pericles knew where the real power lay and played up to it. In doing so, they laid themselves open to the charge of 'demagoguery' from their opponents (*dêmos* 'people' + *agôg*– 'lead on', with a strong implication of 'by the nose' for purposes of self-advantage).

Expert reject

Some background first. Ancient Greek intellectuals argued that the purpose of government was not economic or social, but moral. Since in ancient Athens the citizenry actually *was* the government, this made sense: the morally better they were, the better the results, the theory went (see on Socrates, below). *Dêm-agôgos*, originally purely descriptive, became the label attached to anyone accused of making the people *worse* (see p. 130–2).

The problem is that the label could be attached to anyone. To the historian Thucydides, Pericles was a hero – incorruptible, far-sighted, unmoved by the easy option, the man who always 'knew what was needed'. But to Plato, he was a pure demagogue, who 'made the people lazy and cowardly and chatterers and money-grubbers' by giving them pay for public service and grants for festivals.

Since our views of government today are rather different, and we (after all) have no power, we do not accuse politicians of corrupting us, only themselves. We want to *feel* good: they are the ones who have to *be* good. A second difference is that today's demagogues lean to the right, ancient ones to the left: Pericles gave to the poor, and Roman 'demagogues' like the Gracchi brothers (second century BC) redistributed land. What is common, however, to the accusation of demagoguery down the ages is the accuser's belief that it is wrong to appeal to the people. They do not know what is really in their interests. Only the experts do.

Modern MPs would all nod vigorously in agreement, thinking themselves experts. So would Socrates and Plato, if MPs really *were* experts. Socrates, for example, argued by analogy with crafts, e.g. carpentry, shoe-making, etc. With these it is possible to define exactly what the product is and how it is produced, and there are criteria for determining what a good shoe is. Such a craft can be taught and passed on. Most important of all, one can say who the expert craftsman actually is. So should it be with goodness (morality, virtue). What is a good citizen? How is one produced? And who produces them? And is producing good citizens a skill that can be taught?

But here was the problem. Because Socrates saw goodness as the only true means to happiness, he argued that it was the function of politicians to produce 'good' citizens: since citizens made the decisions, that alone guaranteed a 'good', i.e. successful, state. But the Athenian democratic Assembly, to his bewilderment, never seemed interested in the question of expertise in this area of 'goodness'. Thus, he says, when ship-building is under discussion, anyone who is not a ship-builder is shouted down, however handsome, wealthy or noble. 'But when the government of the country is being debated, any builder, blacksmith or shoemaker, merchant or ship-owner, rich or poor, of good family or none, can have his say.'

Greeks had a genius for asking the right questions. Why should we listen to (say) an actress like Glenda Jackson about politics? Should *she* listen to *us* about acting? Plato would have been especially appalled that a person who had made her reputation through a trivial medium like the cinema, designed to remove us from the real world, should be seen as a fit person to advise us on it (see p. 135).

Pot shot

The Athenians knew and understood these problems. They also knew that they were vulnerable to inconsistency in making policy, especially if two orators, of equally powerful abilities but opposite views, kept pulling the people this way and that. Ostracism was their answer. Every mid-winter, the Athenian Assembly was asked if it wanted to banish anyone. If it did, two months later, without debate, citizens inscribed any name they liked (one name each) on a piece of pottery (*ostrakon*). As long as six thousand valid *ostraka* were collected, the man gaining most votes was sent into exile for ten years, though not in dishonour. He was still allowed, for example, to draw income from his properties, and he returned as a free citizen when his time was up. Thousands of *ostraka* have been dug up, the most famous being a batch of 191 with Themistocles' name inscribed on them by only four separate hands – either deliberate fraud or the anti-Themistocles campaign (c. 470 BC) ensuring that the illiterate did not miss the chance to vote.

The purpose of ostracism seems to have been to defuse situations in

which the Athenians could not make up their mind between propo-
nents of competing policies. Since they recognised that consistency in
policy was in their interests, an ostracism forced a final decision. The
two-month gap between settling for an ostracism and carrying it out
enabled the issues to be properly clarified.

It did not always work. In 416 BC, during the war against Sparta, the
Athenians decided to ostracise either the dove Nicias or the hawk
Alcibiades. One Hyperbolus, however, fancying his chances once one
of them had been exiled, tried to inflame public opinion against both.
As a result, *he* was the one who was ostracised, leaving the two original
candidates still in Athens and the situation unresolved. The Athenians
had just not thought through what they were trying to achieve. It was
the last ever ostracism. Any Lib-Dem leader would surely be prime
candidate if we had such a splendid system here.

Sucking up

Perhaps one of the oddest features of the Athenian democratic system
to our eyes is its handling of legal matters. Traditionally we separate
legislature and executive from the judiciary (though the Lord
Chancellor does straddle them all). But not the Athenians: the people
ruled the law-courts too, and there were no such people as judges or
law-lords telling them what to do. There was, as a result, no police-
force, and no such thing as a state prosecution. All prosecutions were
brought privately. So as today the press, it is said, is the national
watchdog, so the people were the national watchdog of Athens. The
principle was first elucidated by the Athenian statesman and poet
Solon (*c.* 640-560 BC) and it caused as much trouble then as it does now,
for exactly the same reasons.

The jury system Solon developed was entirely private. So in classical
Athens, in the absence of the police or state prosecutors, aggrieved parties brought their own cases and, like defendants, made their speeches
themselves (but they could hire a speech-writer). The jury (hundreds of
males over 30, selected by lot), after listening to both sides, voted to
condemn or acquit without further discussion or guidance. Many
penalties were fixed by law.

But in the absence of a state prosecution, how could offenders who
had not actually harmed any *individual* (e.g. because they had flouted
citizenship laws or defrauded the treasury) be brought to book? This is
where Solon's 'watchdog' principle came in. He argued that 'the best
governed state was one in which those who were not wronged were as

diligent in prosecuting criminals as those who had personally suffered'. So for certain types of offence, the principle was established that 'anyone who wanted to' could bring a case, often with a fixed reward for winning, though to prevent abuse, failure to gain a fifth of the jury's votes resulted in a heavy fine.

It was a nosy-parker's dream. Athenians called such people *sukophantai* (derivation unknown), and they were deeply loathed. The sycophant naturally posed as a public benefactor, arguing high-mindedly that he was only 'serving the national interest' – like newspaper editors, arguing that it is in the 'national interest' that what is private be made public, and Peter Tatchell 'outing' people for their sexuality. But Athenians saw them as interfering busy-bodies with a single end in view, making fast and easy profits out of the innocent (when they were not otherwise trying to break political reputations).

In his comedy *Wealth* (388 BC), the Athenian comic playwright Aristophanes holds up a sycophant to ridicule. The play begins with the blind god Wealth having his sight restored. Since Wealth can now see who deserves to be rich, the sycophant finds himself impoverished. He laments his 'patriotic martyrdom', claiming that, as 'unofficial superintendent of all public and private affairs', he is simply 'seeking to help my beloved city to the utmost of my ability'. But however loathed the sycophant was, at least he was supposed to be on the lookout for crime.

The Roman way

It is worth ending with the Romans. Their republican oligarchy, not Greek democracy, is the source of our system – and far more democratic than ours it is too, for all its Julius Caesars and Pompeys, its consuls and Senate.

The Greek historian Polybius (*c.* 200-118 BC) described Roman government as a combination of kingship, oligarchy and democracy, and thought it was the balance of such a system that explained its success. It worked as follows. The various (and complicated) Assemblies of the people (democracy) elected Rome's magistrates (executive officers, serving for one year, as treasurers, judges, and so on). When their term was up, these magistrates automatically joined in perpetuity the ranks of the advisory body, the Senate (oligarchy). The Senate had no official authority, but it was always consulted and its advice usually taken (it was, after all, an ex-magistrates' club, advising existing magistrates – see p. 116). So it was a very influential body indeed. The top magistrates were the two consuls (kingship). They had very wide powers (such as commanding the army and presiding over the Senate). To reach that exalted position, a man had to work his way up through the various lower magistracies and could not be consul till he was forty-two. But again, a consul, being a magistrate, served for one year only.

So far, so British: it looks as if the Senate and consuls had it all wrapped up, like parliament and the prime minister. But there were two further democratic elements. First, the people elected their own representatives, 'tribunes of the *plebs*', to the Senate, and they could veto any Senate business they chose. Second, all legislation passed by the Senate had to go back to the people to be ratified. It was not enough merely for the Senate to agree to it: the people had to agree to it too before it became law.

One wonders what our great democratic MPs would say if the people *had* to ratify, and *could* veto, all parliamentary legislation. They would without doubt be against it. But then they have always been against democracy. Up to the late nineteenth century, what we now call 'democracy' used to be called 'republicanism' after the Roman and American models, so hateful was the term 'democracy' to politicians. Only recently has the term become fashionable. But the concept is no less distasteful to our masters.

The Greeks invented the idea of people-power: the Romans developed a practical form of it (see p. 85). Indeed, if we believe the Romans, they even got there first: the embryo Republic was established in 509 BC after the rape of Lucretia and subsequent expulsion of the Etruscan kings – two years before Cleisthenes' democratic reforms in Athens.

EUROPEAN RECORDS

On top of keeping a very close eye on our production of sausages, prawn-flavoured crisps and cider, the EC scheme to record every field, sheep, cow, pig, chicken, farm and farmer in the country takes us back into the mists of pre-history.

Homer's epics (eighth century BC) tell of heroes such as Agamemnon and Nestor living in great palaces like Mycenae and Pylos. Excavation has uncovered them and others, in a period we call the Mycenaean age (ending in the eleventh century BC). Among the ruins were found inscribed clay tablets, preserved by being baked hard in the conflagrations that destroyed the palaces. These tablets (called 'Linear B') are a form of Greek, and record a society labelled, inspected, rationed and controlled by an officialdom of a sort to make the heart of any EC bureaucrat beat that little bit faster. Ironically, these cheap clay tablets were temporary records, awaiting transfer to a more 'permanent' material, perhaps skins (as we enter the electronic age, it will be 'temporary' paper documents that survive electronic sabotage).

The tablets tell us the wheat and fig rations for thirty-seven female bath attendants at Pylos; what the acreage of Alektruon's estate is and how much he should pay in annual tax, as well as to Poseidon and Diwieus; that in one palace room there is a single pair of brassbound chariot wheels labelled 'useless'; that in one Cretan village two nurses, one girl and one boy are being employed (Mycenaeans took over Crete in the fifteenth century BC); and that Dunios owes to the palace 2,220 litres of barley, 526 of olives, 468 of wine; 15 rams, 8 yearlings, 1 ewe, 13 he-goats, 12 pigs, 1 fat hog, 1 cow and 2 bulls; that there are oxen called Dusky, Dappled, Whitefoot and Noisy. Above all, sheep dominate the tablets: the total runs to nearly 100,000. Most of them are castrated rams used for producing wool; young and old are carefully listed. Breeding flocks are recorded separately, ewes being listed with their lambs. Wool yield is measured, about 750 g being expected per ram (less for the ewes). No wonder there is no mention of this in Homer. Heroes have better things to do than weigh and record wool yields. But given the form-filling it must have entailed, it is a miracle they launched *one* ship for Troy, let alone a thousand. Can one imagine assembling a European army?

Farce of destiny

As far as Europe goes, we are told time and again that this time there is no looking back: it is 'manifest destiny'. Aristophanes would have resisted the notion. Ever the champion of the Little Guy against Them, he composed *Acharnians*, 'Men from Acharnae', for performance at the comic festival in Athens in January 425 BC. Its hero is Dicaeopolis, 'Honest Citizen', a small farmer who has been forced to live within the walls of Athens as a result of the current war against Sparta. This had begun in 431 BC and looked like going on for ever. Dicaeopolis is sick of the war, hates the city and yearns for peace and his farm and his village. He is always first at the democratic Assembly of citizens, demanding debates about peace – in vain.

Tiring of the charade, Dicaeopolis decides to take his 'manifest destiny' in his own hands. He persuades the god Amphitheus to go to Sparta and conclude a thirty-year truce on a purely private basis between himself and the Spartans. He is attacked for this by the Acharnians, men who want to fight the Spartans to the death, but he manages to win them to his side. Dicaeopolis now establishes his farm as a private market within which he trades freely with enemy nations. The goods of Greece pour into his household, while Athenians, informers, war-mongers and other parasites seeking to share his good fortune are given short shrift. At the end of the comedy a randy and drunken Dicaeopolis reels on after a party organised by the priest of Dionysus, god of drama, while the self-important General Lamachus, just returned from fighting, limps away wounded from a raid. The Little Guy has triumphed again.

We need an EC-free area, where trade really *is* free, Turkish cigarettes compulsory, Australian butter and New Zealand lamb on every table, and any shape, size or style of apple allowed. Rutland?

In his comedy *Birds* (414 BC), Aristophanes returns to the theme of escape from present lunacies to a better world (cf. p. 4). The comedy opens with Peisetairos and Euelpides leaving Athens in search of a new city. Their complaint is that in Athens one cannot move for lawsuits. All they want to do is find a place where they can settle down and live in peace, free from litigation and its fees and fines. They hope to persuade one of the birds to identify from the air a suitable place to move to, but when no such place emerges, Peisetairos has a brilliant idea: why not found a new city, with the birds, up in the sky? Whence 'Cloudcuckooland', the name invented for this brave new world.

But as soon as the birds start building it, along come legions of busy-bodies from the earth below determined to put in the oar of officialdom: a priest, set on overseeing the foundation rites, a poet who insists on singing the praises of the city in return (of course) for patronage, a seller of oracles, a town-planner ('Now: the market-place will go *here*, and the radial roads here and *here* ...'), an inspector, and a statute-seller with a stack of bye-laws and regulations to sell to the new city ('Article 6: Cloudcuckoovian Weights, Measures and Currency ...'). Angrily, Peisetairos drives off these parasites in a flurry of beatings and abuse. The city built, Peisetairos uses it to starve out the gods by cutting them off from the savour of sacrifice rising from the earth. They hand him sovereignty, and the play ends in triumph.

Starving out the bureaucrats in Strasbourg and Brussels would make a fine Aristophanic comedy. It would be named after its hostile chorus, as usual: *The Cod-Fishers*? As for the European Central Bank, ancient Greeks would simply not have believed that any people that called itself free would submit to the diktat of an unelected body of bankers

(*bankers*!) that will receive instructions from no one, and have total and exclusive control over the monetary affairs of all member countries, with the absolute right to interfere, at will, when they so decide.

Eurotrash

Even in telling us to clean up our water supply, the EC gets it wrong, though it is at least exhibiting a thoroughly classical concern. Most Greek cities got their water from public fountains fed by local springs. Greek doctors new to a district examined the supply to determine likely ailments (one spring was said to make your teeth fall out). A few towns had piped supplies: Athens for one (some thought Spartans poisoned it to cause the terrible plague of 431 BC which killed thousands including Pericles) and Greek Pergamum (in Turkey), from a source 20 miles away. An inscription there orders wardens to ensure 'fountains are clean and that pipes supplying them allow the free flow of water'.

The Romans were the great water engineers, spreading comfort and luxury thereby far down the social scale. The first aqueduct was commissioned in Rome in 312 BC. The four aqueducts serving provincial Lyon produced 17 million gallons of water a day, from pipes up to 47 miles long. Rome in the fourth century AD had, according to a survey, 154 public lavatories, 856 bath buildings, and 1,352 water points (and 46 brothels). Such projects brought tremendous prestige to donors. The water came into reservoirs with settling tanks, taps and sluices, and citizens who had it piped from the public main into their private homes were a major source of revenue. The Roman architect Vitruvius (first century BC) gives rules for checking its cleanliness at source: are the inhabitants there strong, without physical distortions or inflamed eyes? Does the water leave traces when sprinkled over certain alloy vessels? When boiled in a copper pan, does it leave a sludge? Will it cook vegetables quickly? Is it clear, from an untainted source? Vitruvius knew that lead pipes were unhealthy ('observe the lead workers' pallid complexion'), but scholars doubt lead poisoning caused the fall of the Roman Empire. The point here is that provincials often appealed to the emperor for help. The emperor never imposed 'help' on provincials.

A Roman Europe

This surely *is* the point. As European ministers never cease to point out, EMU cannot possibly work unless a single, central policy, imposed on all national interests, drives it. This was not the Roman way.

There is no doubt that the purpose of the Roman empire (*c.* 240 BC – AD 400 in the west, longer in the east) was to maintain Rome – its emperor, army, city and *auctoritas* – in the fashion to which it had become accustomed. There is equally no doubt that the provinces did this by forcibly paying taxes and providing bases and men for Rome's legions. Responsibility for all this was devolved downwards from the emperor (who set Rome's financial and military targets) to his provincial governors, and they in turn devolved it on to the province's regions. A region's local, wealthy élite was the key. Rome's first move in creating a new province was always to offer the élite plum administrative jobs, hand in hand with an impressive, sustained programme of urban rebuilding on a Roman scale (forums, temples, baths, theatres, aqueducts and so on). With the élite's support won by such irresistible packages, the rest of the provincials living in the cities (the places that really counted) could be expected to play along. As far as compulsion goes, that was just about it.

At the same time, there were undoubted advantages for the provincials in submitting to Rome. With due exceptions, membership of the empire was of broad economic, social and cultural benefit. Rome did not interfere with religious practices or with local structures or institutions. They did not impose their own coinage or economic or even legal norms. The various systems knocked along side by side, though inevitably the Roman way of doing things (especially in relation to the law and coinage) tended to become the norm. The point is that the empire *had* to work largely by consensus between Rome and the locals. There were not enough Romans to go round controlling every aspect of provincials' lives. That it did work for so long suggests the Roman formula was about right. Interestingly, only the bolshy Brits required permanent standing legions in place throughout Britain's history as a province.

But the EC is a quite different style of organisation, and as EMU gets under way, one senses the prison doors closing. One wonders who the tenant of the new Imperial Palace in Brussels will be, and whom he or she will appoint as provincial governors with their iron mandates. One can already sense the Widmerpools rising effortlessly without trace to claim the prizes. A hot tip for EC provincial governor of the UK is surely the eternally unelectable Neil Kinnock. What scintillating courts of hand-picked élites he and the lovely Glenys would gather round them in London and the regions in opposition to parliament! Come on, you bolshy Brits.

Out-Europing Europe

In fact, of course, every sensible Englishman is entirely in favour of Europeans. We want to drink their delicious wines, eat their scrumptious food, travel on their wonderful railways, speak their heavenly languages, and sit in their glorious sunshine, talking drivel. We just don't want to be told what to do by the brutes. It may be that we could subvert the whole enterprise by playing the Roman ourselves.

For all his name, Lucius Cornelius Balbus was in Roman eyes a foreigner. He came from Cadiz in Spain, and was a Phoenician, of semitic origin. After noble service in the Roman army in Spain, however, he was rewarded with Roman citizenship in 72 BC, and formed a close connection with Julius Caesar, serving on his senior staff both in Spain and later in Gaul. But in 56 BC political enemies in Rome attempted to strip him of his citizenship, and the orator-politician Cicero came to his defence.

Cicero argues that it is absurd that the Roman people should offer citizenship to those they have defeated in battle but withhold it from those who have supported the Roman cause. He lays it down as a general principle that there is no community in the world, whether hostile or affectionate to Rome, whose individual members should not be allowed to enjoy Roman citizenship, circumstances permitting. Further, he points out that their ancestors laid it down that it was impossible for anyone to be forced on to or ejected off the citizens' roll without that person's express permission. He goes on to say that one of the main reasons for the greatness and glory of the Roman nation was the willingness of the Roman people to open the doors of citizenship even to enemies, and welcome them in. Cicero quotes the old Roman poet Ennius, who made Hannibal say 'Any man who smites our enemy shall be, as far as I am concerned, a Carthaginian, whoever he is, and whatever his country' (cf. Henry V, of anyone who fights with him at Agincourt – 'be he ne'er so vile, this day shall gentle his condition').

So we should avoid EMU by over-trumping the EC and turning ourselves (rather than Brussels) into the Romans. Let us magnanimously offer English citizenship automatically to all Europeans, giving them precisely the same privileges and status here as any Englishman. We can even give them the vote: they can vote to fill the House of Lords, turning that body into our one European political connection.

VOTER ROTA

Political parties today try to win elections with on-the-hoof policies which they hope will forge a polling-day bond with an electorate ignored for the previous and the subsequent five years. In ancient Rome, Mafia-like networks of pre-existing bonds and obligations between powerful families and friends held the key to electoral success.

The 2,800 election notices from Pompeii (overwhelmed by Vesuvius in AD 79), hand-painted in red on house walls, show the system at work. They are personal ('I ask you to support A', 'B urges you to support C for office'), with very few references to policy or interest groups (one reads 'The Late Drinkers support Vatia for aedile' – surely a joke. Was Vatia one for the bottle?). The notices cluster along main streets and around candidates' homes, and analysis suggests they were not posted at whim, but organised by the candidates themselves. They highlight the strength of the personal bond between candidate and support.

Where obligation is the key, policy is largely irrelevant. This comes out well in 'The Short Guide to Electioneering', a pamphlet Quintus Cicero wrote for his brother, *the* Cicero, when he was standing for consul in 63 BC. Of non-consular family, the 'new boy' Cicero needed to work doubly hard to win. Quintus stresses that he must ask those he has already helped as a lawyer to repay their obligation to him now, assure the powerful that they will not regret supporting him, and make friends where he normally would not. Policy never appears. Cicero won, and was soon composing 'letters of support' for friends seeking influential positions.

We know parties and MPs forge private bonds of obligation with business and unions. The electorate is never consulted. If your MP ever solicits your vote, put on your best godfather voice and say 'Why do you come to me *now*?'

Public interest

It might also be worth asking your MP if secret ballots are such a good idea. The Romans were not so certain. All voting had been carried out by open, public ballot till the *lex Gabinia* of 139 BC introduced secret voting for the people to elect executive officials (praetor, consul, etc). The practice then spread to all voting (e.g. in trials and for the passing of laws). The argument against secret voting, says Cicero, is that it enables mischievous people to keep the reasons for their decisions

secret, and honourable people from showing whom they have supported and thus gaining the credit from them. Cicero proposes a
compromise – secret voting, but the ballots are to be made available for
inspection by the upper classes. It did not catch on.

The younger Pliny, a provincial governor writing under the Empire
a hundred years later, takes up the issue in two of his letters. By now
the Senate (not the people) was electing officials by open voting, but
the procedure had become so chaotic and personal influence so strong
that a secret ballot was introduced again. Pliny admits this has been
working successfully for the moment, but is afraid that it will not last.
In a later letter Pliny proudly declares he was right. 'At the recent election, some of the voting papers were found to have jokes and
obscenities scribbled on them ... this is the confidence that unprincipled characters derive from the assurance that "no one will know".'

But what is Pliny's explanation of the reason why people have
behaved like this? His reasoning is the very reverse of ours: 'very few
people are as scrupulously honest in secret as they are in public, and
many are influenced by public opinion but very few by conscience'. In
other words, for Pliny, the public stage was the true test of a man. He
goes on 'if a man by secret voting can play ribald tricks with his ballot
paper in an important matter on such a serious occasion, what are we
to suppose his private conduct to be?' Bring back public voting?

Listen or lump it

As soon as a party nowadays is elected, it at once makes pious declara-
tions about 'serving the people'. Weasel words, of course. Interestingly,
Roman emperors really did know about serving the people. Hadrian
(emperor AD 117-138) was on his travels abroad when a woman came
up to him, took hold of his toga and demanded to be heard. Hadrian
shook her off, saying he was too busy. She shouted 'In that case, do not
be emperor!' Hadrian stopped and listened.

It is an astonishing fact that the Roman emperor, controlling territory that stretched from Britain to Syria, from the Rhine to Egypt, was
personally involved at every level of decision-making throughout the
empire, from the grandest embassy to the humblest individual.
Imperial correspondence, for example, came direct to the emperor.
Trajan (emperor AD 98-117) once acceded to the request of a centurion
for citizenship for his daughter in a letter that had been pinned to one
from the provincial governor Pliny the younger. Imperial hearings to
administer personal appeals for justice continued even when the

emperor was on campaign or his travels. Written petitions were frequently presented by hand. Many of these were from women on family matters. Marcus Aurelius (emperor AD 161-180), for example, informed a woman illegally married for forty years to her uncle that, in view of the circumstances, her children would be deemed legitimate. And so, interminably, on.

This left very little time for actual policy making. The first emperor Augustus was an exception, but later emperors appeared to spend most of their time responding to their subjects, who came to expect a personal reply to their personal problems (and usually got one). This is not to say that emperors never initiated change, just that change was not a normal or expected function. Not the way our PMs behave, more's the pity.

In Cabinet circles

The next thing a newly elected party does is to appoint its ministerial teams both in and out of Cabinet, but (as they well know, or will soon find out) they are of no importance. PMs tend to win elections their way, and the PM's teams will do as they are told, or else. It is in the faithful inner ring, like the Roman emperors' 'court', where, to everyone's fury, the real business will be done.

Roman historians such as Tacitus (*c.* AD 56-120) and Dio Cassius (AD 150-235) found this propensity for secrecy exasperating as they attempted to describe the workings of empire. All they essentially had to go on was rumour. Dio puts it well, pointing out that under the republic all decisions were taken by the Senate and people and made a matter of record. But under the emperors, 'even though some things are made public by chance, they are not believed because they cannot be verified. People suspect that things are said and done in accordance with the wishes of the men in power and their associates. As a result, much that is false becomes common currency and much that is true remains hidden from sight, and in nearly every case a version of events gains ground that is different from the way it really happened.'

So the interesting question for a Roman was – who could reach the ear of the emperor, and under what conditions? It was his inner ring that controlled access, and it could include wives, mistresses, children and even freed slaves. Pallas, for example, one of the most influential freedmen in the court of Claudius (emperor AD 41-54), began life as the slave of Claudius' mother Antonia. On some occasions, an emperor's inner ring would consist of just one man. Tiberius (emperor AD 14-37), for example, fell under the spell of a particularly nasty piece of work, Lucius Aelius Sejanus, captain of the Praetorian Guard.

Tacitus ascribes Sejanus' rise to power to a combination of long-term intrigue and the gods' hatred of Rome. Sejanus, he tells us, was not of senatorial family. He made money as a young man by a sexual liason with a wealthy Roman debauchee, and as captain of the Guard slowly wormed his way into Tiberius' good books. After the death of Tiberius' son in AD 23 (Sejanus was said to have poisoned him), he began to wield unhealthy influence over the emperor and started to get rid of his opponents by exile or imprisonment. In AD 26 Sejanus advised Tiberius to leave Rome for Capri, and became even more powerful. He was elected consul in AD 31 and all seemed set fair for him either to stage a coup or cement his place in the imperial succession when he was suddenly revealed in his true colours. Tiberius, acting with terrifying decisiveness, had Sejanus, his adherents and even children executed. His body, apparently, was torn to pieces by his enemies and thrown into the Tiber.

Tacitus' summary of the man is telling. Ambitious, indefatigable, Sejanus was 'secretive about himself, an incriminator of others, servility and arrogance side by side; outwardly modest and composed, inwardly lusting passionately for power; sometimes extravagant and self-indulgent, more often hard-working and watchful – which is as damaging as excess, when the throne is its aim.' No fear of any such individual emerging out of the ranks of a modern government's deliciously loyal inner ring, of course.

Eunuch power'll do

But just in case the PM is worried, Cyrus the Great (559-529 BC), king of Persia, had some useful thoughts on the subject of loyalty in the ranks. His biographer, Xenophon, tells us that Cyrus realised the scale of the problem he faced after he had taken Babylon (539 BC) and decided to proclaim himself king. He was 'about to rule over many people, in the greatest and most famous of all cities, and yet the city was as hostile as any city could be to one man'. He therefore decided he needed a bodyguard, but that, as he saw, solved nothing unless their undying fidelity could be guaranteed.

Cyrus began by reasoning that 'no one was ever faithful who loved someone else better'. So he at once discounted those who had wives or children or male lovers, since such would be bound to put love for them above love for him. That left only one possible group: eunuchs.

It was a brilliant inspiration. Being generally despised, they badly needed a patron – who better than the king, and what better guarantee of loyalty? Likewise, by analogy with animals, they were no weaker nor less efficient for their condition, just less unruly; and 'no one ever performed acts of greater fidelity in their master's misfortunes than eunuchs'. As the PM flicks through his list of loyal colleagues, one wonders whom he has in mind to go under the knife first. Any volunteers?

MPerfection

Given the impossibility, however, of *us* having any real say in whom we get as MP (we just vote for the brutes presented to us by the parties) we all want to know how we can choose the least bad one. The Greek essayist Plutarch gives many useful hints in his 'Rules for politicians'.

First, the decision to enter public life must not be based on 'lack of anything else to do', otherwise the politician is like someone who sails in boats for the fun of it and finds himself swept out to sea, hanging over the side being sea-sick. Desire for fame is equally unproductive: you end up like actors, either the servant of those you hoped to control, or offending those you hoped to please. In fine, politics is like a well: if you fall in thoughtlessly, you will regret it, but if you descend carefully and under control, you will make reasonable use of the situation.

Rational conviction that the work is noble and right for you is the one reason for entering politics. At this point the budding politician must get to know the character of his fellow citizens. Without understanding that, he cannot hope to shape and change them. The politician must modify his own character too: 'men in public life are responsible for more than their public words and actions: their dinners, beds, marriage, amusements and interests are all objects of curiosity'. Plutarch would have made a first-rate tabloid newspaper editor.

Plutarch is especially good on the usefulness of disagreement. It carries conviction among the voters, Plutarch argues, when in large policy matters, party members should at first disagree and then change their minds. It looks as if they are acting from principle. In small matters, however, they should be genuinely allowed to disagree, because then their agreement in important matters does not look pre-concerted. So there is advantage to be gained from controlled party splits. Not many spin doctors know that.

As Plutarch shrewdly pointed out, MPs would do well to try to understand us. The Lib-Dem leader Paddy Ashdown recently proposed to find out what people 'really' wanted from politicians by abandoning his parliamentary duties for three days every week and taking a number of lowly jobs up and down the country.

Greeks and Romans too consulted public opinion, but rather differently from Mr Ashdown. Knowing that, if they were recognised, their chances of getting an honest response were nil, they concealed their identity. So when the greatest sculptor of the Greek world, Pheidias (fifth century BC), wanted to know what people thought of his latest effort, he hid in his studio and listened to their comments – not a course of action one would recommend to modern artists (as if they were interested in what the public thought anyway). Germanicus, the popular adopted son of the Roman emperor Tiberius, on campaign in Germany in AD 14, dressed himself in an animal-skin and wandered among his soldiers to ascertain morale, like Shakespeare's Henry V before Agincourt.

Others had less reputable motives. The Roman historian Suetonius (b. *c.* AD 70) tells us that Nero donned disguise to prowl the streets, taverns and brothels of Rome by night, murdering passers-by and dropping them down the sewers, breaking into shops, and molesting senators' wives (on one occasion he was caught and severely beaten). He visited the theatre in disguise during the afternoon, joining in the fun by pelting the crowd from his position high above the stage when fights between rival groups of actors broke out.

One is not suggesting this is what Mr Ashdown had in mind. But he would have done well to read Plutarch's treatise 'On Distinguishing Flatterers from Friends' before he set out. Politicians are notoriously prone to self-love, and self-love, as Plutarch says, leads to self-deception. This presents the flatterer with the perfect launch-pad. Wander the streets in disguise if you want to hear the truth, Mr Ashdown.

Opium and circuses

But it is not long these days before it becomes transparent that the newly elected party has no more idea what it is doing than the previous lot did – only it is now under the considerable disadvantage of having to do it. One's thoughts turn to how the Roman emperors would have handled the situation. The orator and public servant Cornelius Fronto (*c.* AD 95-166) has some useful advice, gleaned from his observation of the emperor Trajan.

Because of his shrewd understanding of the people, Fronto points

out, Trajan paid close attention to the stage, the horses and the gladiatorial arena. He was aware that the people were controlled principally
by two things – free grain and shows (bread and circuses, as the satirist
Juvenal put it) – and that political support depended as much on entertainment as on the serious business of running the state. General
popularity was politically as important as effective policy.

Fronto goes on to say that Trajan knew that there was an important
distinction to be made here between bread (i.e. free grain, the dole,
handouts) and public shows. The point was that hand-outs were less
effective than shows because they placated only those who qualified
for them; but the whole people, rich and poor alike, adored shows and
could therefore be won over by going to see them. So when in AD 108
Trajan celebrated the military victories he had won in Dacia (northern
Romania), he put on 117 days of entertainment in Rome at which ten
thousand gladiators (see p. 150) fought and eleven thousand animals
were killed. Mind-numbing TV spectaculars – that is what the people
want (cf. p. 109). The only hope for the Millennium Dome is that it is
seen as the first tottering step down that road.

A.m. PM, p.m. tyrant

As the ruling party becomes even more unpopular and even more des-
perately tries to find out either what it thinks or what the people want,
so the reputation of the PM gradually declines – just like poor old
Pompey's did. In 59 BC Rome was effectively in the grip of a trium-
virate of Caesar, Crassus and Pompey, but Pompey had fallen
disastrously out of favour. Cicero wrote in a letter about him:

> And now there is our poor old friend, unused to being out of
> favour, always basking in praise and bathed in glory, now literally
> shrunken and broken in spirit … In front, he sees the cliff-edge,
> behind the accusation of U-turns. I saw him recently addressing
> a public meeting. How proudly he once used to dominate that
> stage, loved by all, everyone's favourite! How abject and con-
> temptible he was then, as pathetic a figure in his own eyes as
> much as his audience's. What a sight! Fallen from the heights, he
> looked like a man who had been pushed rather than jumped.

Herodotus records how the Persian Darius (to become king of Persia
in 521 BC) put his finger on the problem of oligarchies like ours: 'the
fact that a number of men are competing for distinction in public ser-

vice cannot but lead to violent personal feuds. Each of them wants to get to the top and see his own proposals carried; so they quarrel. This leads to open dissension, then bloodshed. The only way to get things back on an even keel again is a return to monarchy – which goes to show how superior monarchy is.' In other words, there is always bloodshed if someone does not decide who the leader really is.

Our oligarchy is becoming increasingly tyrannical, as Mr Blair and Mrs Thatcher know only too well. Plato would agree, pointing out that he mapped the path to tyranny long ago. Towards the end of his *Republic*, having discussed the nature of the ideal society, he describes how societies deteriorate, and uses this as an image of how individuals can be corrupted. He shows how the best (aristocracy) can be compromised by e.g. love of money; how money takes over their lives completely, and the wealthy few emerge on top (oligarchy); and how mass resentment drives the people to expel the oligarchs and claim power for themselves (democracy), where life degenerates into a lawless free-for-all, anything goes, and 'everyone is treated equally, whether they are or not'.

What happens next, according to Plato, is that because this 'equal' society still possesses rich and poor, the poor select a champion who makes himself tyrant. At first, 'he greets everyone with a smile, claims to be no tyrant, makes lots of promises, and poses as an amiable and gentle person'. Then he settles his differences with some of his enemies and kills others, and provokes warfare 'so as to keep people in need of a leader'. Meanwhile, he keeps an eye out for men of courage, intelligence and wealth and eliminates them. Then he surrounds himself with a cabinet of admirers 'while decent people avoid him like the plague' ... but one hardly needs continue.

But then Plato was never sure about politics or politicians anyway. In his dialogue *Gorgias* he raises the question: what is a politician for? Should he aim to gratify people's desires by offering them what is pleasant? Or should he be concerned only with their real welfare, however painful? He puts in Socrates' mouth the famous analogy of the doctor brought to trial against a pastry-cook before a jury of children:

Socrates: Just imagine, how would a doctor defend himself if he were hauled up before some children, and the pastry-cook accused him as follows? 'Children, this man has done the most awful things to you. He messes up the youngest of you by cutting and burning; he reduces you to skeletons and chokes you, giving you horrible, bitter medicines till you do not know whether you are coming or going, and forces you to go without food and drink – not like me, eh? I gave you the most delicious feasts, didn't I?'

What do you think a doctor trapped in this miserable situation would have to say? Or what if he told them the truth and said 'All this, children, I did for your own good' – what sort of outcry do you think that reply would draw from the jury? A pretty big one, wouldn't you think?

And Socrates goes on to re-affirm the position he has held throughout the dialogue: that the very worst thing a man can do is injustice. Indeed, he goes on to say, were he ever to be brought to court, he would be happy to be condemned to death if he had based his case not on attempts to flatter the jurors but only on what was just. But 'justice' does not have a very sexy, vote-winning ring to it.

Promises to keep

But then, whatever promises a politician makes, it is a racing certainty that they will be broken sooner or later. How can we keep them up to the mark? It is worth here remembering the Roman Regulus, who, captured by the Carthaginians in 255 BC, was sent to Rome to make peace but only after swearing an oath to return if he failed. He ordered the Romans not to negotiate, returned, and was tortured to death. Since it is obviously not worth putting politicians on their honour, should we put them under oath? If so, the ancient Greek model would be a good one.

Gods were called upon to witness ancient oaths, not because gods were righteous but because they would be dishonoured if an oath sealed in their name were broken. The oath was accompanied by libations of wine and an animal sacrifice. The animal victim was dismembered, hands were plunged into bowls of its blood, and the oath-takers stood on its severed sexual organs to seal the compact. This was an awesome and terrifying ceremony. One longs to see Tony Benn performing it. The accompanying act of self-cursing was equally grim. In Homer's *Iliad* the formula runs 'whoever is first to break this oath, let his brains run into the ground like this wine'. In classical times, Greeks prayed that the oath-breaker and his whole family should be wiped out.

In a culture where there were no paper transactions to provide records or proof, it was vital to have such means to guarantee that a promise was binding. So oaths commonly accompanied all commercial, military and legal transactions. The Greek politician Lycurgus (fourth century BC), who understood about social fabric, said 'It is the oath that keeps our democracy together'; when a character in a Euripides' tragedy said 'It was my tongue that swore, not my heart', it was used as evidence of Euripides' gross immorality. Who was it who recently said 'Read my lips: no more taxes'?

BUYING POWER

Our MPs put up a valiant fight a few years ago but eventually agreed to Lord Nolan's report that they would have to disclose all their earnings. The ancients would have found this very strange: why did they not *long* to reveal all?

Ancient Greeks took the view that the richer you were, the less likely you were to be corruptible. There was thus a tendency to appoint only the very wealthy to positions such as e.g. custodianship of temple treasures, since they would be less tempted to pilfer. The millionaire Roman Gaius Asinius Gallus took a different line. The Roman historian Tacitus (*c.* AD 56-120) reports that, when some senators discussed restricting displays of material wealth, Gallus replied that senators and the rich were a special case. They were not intrinsically different from others, he said, but because of their precedence in station, rank and honours 'they needed special provision for their mental and physical well-being. Otherwise, leading men would have all the worries and dangers, and none of the compensations.' There was truth in this. Any Roman who wanted to become consul needed vast sums of money to buy popularity and votes. The accepted way to do this was to sponsor extravagant gladiatorial games (mass slaughter of men and exotic animals) and generous grain hand-outs for the urban poor. This required a huge income – or vast debt, of the sort Caesar saddled himself with during his early climb up the career ladder.

The Romans, of course, did these things properly. Caesar and Pompey, for example, picked up a cool £50 million for ratifying Cleopatra's father Ptolemy XII as king of Egypt in 59 BC. Caesar's campaigns in Gaul (58-51 BC) netted him a second fortune. Provincial governors, appointed from ex-magistrates, could make millions, by foul means or fair. They had to. As Roman wits said, a governor had to make three fortunes to survive: one to recoup election expenses incurred while climbing up the ladder in Rome, one to bribe the jury on charges of provincial mismanagement, and one to live off thereafter.

Gaius Verres, for example, the corrupt governor of Rome's oldest province Sicily, whom Cicero prosecuted at the Sicilians' request in 70 BC, was a tabloid's dream. He had a taste for fine art, so temples were plundered for their statues and citizens for their silverware. One for the women, he had them procured for him wherever he went – including virgin daughters of distinguished citizens. Since cities that wanted to avoid contributing money for the defence of Sicily simply bribed Verres to let them off, the navy was a shambles. Fancying the wife of one Cleomenes, Verres put Cleomenes in charge of this 'fleet', which was promptly routed and fired by a pirate ship, watched by the whole population. The pirates then took an unhindered leisure-tour of the harbour at Syracuse. Finally, Verres subjected even Roman citizens to torture and death without trial – one was even crucified.

Today's sleaze seems very feeble by comparison. But the issue was not just Verres' crimes: it concerned the standing of the Roman Senate. Verres was to be tried by a Senatorial court, and Cicero began his prosecution by saying that the word on the street was that no one with influence (i.e. money) would ever be found guilty in such an arena. In other words, it was the Senate's authority and reputation that were on the line. So, surely, today.

Brown envelopes

The problem is nicely focussed by the Roman word for bribery, *ambitus*. It is cognate with the word for 'going round canvassing for votes', *ambitio* (whence our 'ambition'). The two went hand in hand. Gift-exchange was the oil which kept the wheels of life rolling sweetly. It was the way by which all relationships – social, political or business – were sealed. The agreement being reciprocal, it was the height of rudeness not to respond to a gift with one in return.

Since, then, bribery did not necessarily imply 'corruption', politicians happily dispensed goodies to cultivate the public, and Romans were not much worried by it. They understood about bread and circuses. For the public, too, palm-greasing was the easiest way of cutting through red tape to reach officials, and in such cases officials probably heeded the maxim of the emperor Caracalla (AD 198-217), to be careful to take 'neither everything, nor every time, nor from every one'. Penalties for even extreme cases of palm-greasing were never severe.

It was a different matter, however, when people found themselves defrauded by those whose help they bought. Verconius Turinus was attached to the court of Severus Alexander (Roman emperor AD 222-

235). Turinus put it about that the emperor was in his pocket, and as a result took massive sums in bribes from those who thought he could influence (for example) decisions in law-suits and placements for commands or provincial governorships. The Romans called it 'selling smoke' (*fumum vendere*). When Severus heard of it, he constructed an elaborate trick involving a hoax petitioner. Turinus duly fell for it, and was revealed in his true colours. Severus ordered him to be bound to a stake in a public forum, and a fire of straw and wet logs was constructed around him. There he was suffocated to death by the smoke, while the herald cried 'He who sold smoke is punished by smoke'. All this makes brown envelopes look pathetic. It also makes one think about the behaviour of parties dispensing hand-outs and promises (rarely fulfilled) to the people in election years. Very Roman behaviour in our Anglo-Saxon culture, which on the whole rather disapproves of public gift-giving.

Gifting a bribe

Ancient Greeks also knew all about political 'gifts'. The fifth-century BC comic poet Cratinus was moved to invent three mock goddesses of bribery: *Doro*, St Give, *Dexo*, St Receive and *Emblo*, St Backhander. You could bribe your way into positions of political or executive power, to start a war or bring peace, to secure citizen rights or a legacy, to prevent or win a legal action, to stop a proposal going to the Assembly, to gain a favourable oracle, and so on and on. But, as with the Romans, the issue was whether corruption was involved. Courts dealing with such cases bandied about terms like 'corruption' and metaphors from the despised world of trade ('buying', 'selling' 'profit' and so on). Outside the courts, however, it was more usually described as 'giving', 'receiving' and 'persuading'.

Another angle on the problem was the normal practice of the wealthy to enhance their reputations – or shore them up? – by magnanimous public gestures e.g. providing the cash to build a library or a school (see p. 103ff.). Here was a transparent public benefit. The fifth-century BC thinker Democritus argues that there is nothing like the rich giving to the poor to produce concord that strengthens the community. The Greek orator Hyperides (389-322 BC) even points out to the Athenians that they allow statesman and soldiers to make large 'personal profits', provided they 'are used in your interests, not against them'. Even here, there was an exception. The one no-go area even for Athenians was private deals with non-Athenians, outsiders. The people, judge and jury of all political matters in ancient Athens, saw such a relationship as a serious threat to their own community.

Romans, however, were far more relaxed about outsider trading. Rulers of a mighty empire, they expected their great men to do deals with the wealthy elsewhere, whoever they were. But moralists like Cicero (first century BC) were fiercely opposed to any signs of avarice in Rome's leaders. Cicero cited the story of Manius Curius, a famous Roman general who was found cooking up his usual dish of turnips when Sabine clients, bearing legitimate gifts to the man who was their patron, approached him. He imperiously dismissed them, saying it was better to defeat the rich than be rich. 'No vice is more foul than avarice among leaders of men', Cicero thunders elsewhere. 'There is nothing by which those in charge of public affairs can more easily endear themselves to the masses than by incorruptible abstemiousness.' Meanwhile our wonderful MPs continue to award themselves and their advisers rises in the shape of the first sum of money that comes to mind, irrespective of the guidelines they lay down for everyone else.

Third world

If the Roman empire had its villains, it had its heroes too. The third world, for example, needs a cohort of Pliny the youngers (*c.* AD 61-112). Debts run up by these countries are now unmanageable, and the cry is to cancel them. But they were legally entered into; and too much of the money was wasted on vast, corrupt bureaucracies anyway. But if one does not cancel them, how do the countries make progress? Enter Pliny.

Ancient Italy, like most of the third world, was essentially an agricultural subsistence economy – a nation of farmers working the land to live off it and create a small surplus with which to 'buy in' the other services they needed. Those who did not possess their own smallholding turned to renting it from the big landowners like Pliny, the real rich of the ancient world.

In his letters, Pliny describes how he handles some of the problems. On one occasion he relates how, despite reducing the rent to tenant farmers (perhaps because of a run of bad harvests – Pliny is not specific), arrears continued to build up to the point where the tenants had lost any hope of repaying them and simply consumed what they produced there and then. Pliny could have ejected the tenants, but he chose instead to receive payment not in cash but in a share of the produce. On another occasion, he sold to contractors the rights to pick and sell his grape harvest while it was still on the vine 'and prospects seemed good'. But the harvest failed, threatening the contractors with ruin. Far from leaving them in the lurch, however, Pliny established a complex system of rebates to those who had put up the money.

The point about these two cases is that, for all his wealth, Pliny was still dependent on those who worked his land. If they failed or went bankrupt for any reason, it left him with a problem – finding new, and not necessarily better, tenants, or new contractors (with all the local unpopularity he might thus incur). As he says of the latter, his rebates 'seemed a suitable way of expressing my gratitude for their past services, and of encouraging them not only to buy from me in the future but also to pay their debts'. Debt cancellation in the third world is in everyone's interest – as long as there are enough Pliny the youngers to oversee the situation in the first place.

Cash limits

The gay abandon with which MPs cancel their own debts, hiking their salaries and expenses whenever they feel like it, contrasts strongly with the behaviour of the inventors of democracy. For all Plato and Aristotle's contempt (because the Assembly, not the law, was sovereign), Athenian radical democracy exhibited considerable self-restraint. The Assembly could have put in train land-redistribution, for example, welfarism, and other manifestations of rampant socialism. It never did. When the silver mines at Laurium in southern Attica started coming good in the 480s BC, for example, there was a proposal in the Assembly to distribute it all among the citizens, but Themistocles' far more intelligent suggestion to build a fleet (and so an empire) with it carried the day, and created serious wealth for public consumption for many years to come. Even more surprising, while Pericles introduced pay for service in the law-courts, the pay was worth only about half of what a casual labourer could have earned, and its value consistently fell. But the Assembly never took advantage of its absolute power to vote enormous increases for itself. It was a truly conservative body. The contrast with our MPs' ruthless exploitation of their position is striking.

Rome was a 'democracy' more in our sense (see p. 80), but even then the Roman people would have been appalled at the idea that the state should provide public money to its senators, and at a level they could choose for themselves, to help them extend their *own* power and influence. That was the senators' personal responsibility, and many fulfilled it by sponsoring public projects on a grand scale out of their own pockets. Corruption was as rife in the ancient world as it is in ours, but at least it was not legalised. Let MPs submit their pay and expense claims to a people's referendum.

Power corrupts

Plato, inevitably, would have deprived MPs of all their worldly wealth. In his *Republic*, Plato describes an ideal, unrealisable society, ruled by 'Guardians', who achieve that status only after a life-time of education and dedication to the best interests of the community (see pp. 11, 124). But Plato is still worried that, for all their training, they may yet become bad apples. He sees their life-style as crucial in keeping them on the straight and narrow. So 'none of them is to have any property, except what is absolutely indispensable, nor living-quarters or store-rooms which are not able to be entered by anyone else. Their stipend is to be their provisions, so fixed that at the end of the year there is no excess or shortfall. They will share mess-halls and their lives will be communal ... further, unlike their fellow citizens, they will have no contact with gold or silver. They are not to wear it or drink from it.'

Plato fears material possessions will corrupt his rulers: 'if they own homes and land and money, they will turn into enemies rather than allies of the community.' But will not this make the Guardians unhappy? Tough, Plato replies: the happiness of the whole community, not just one small part of it, is at stake here. Corrupt Guardians will corrupt the whole state. In that light, maximising the Guardians' happiness is irrelevant. Besides, when the whole state is run properly, it will be happy – and they, therefore, will be happy too. Plato would have banished MPs from the Houses of Parliament and lodged them in the halls of residence in one of our dimmer provincial universities.

The public servant Pliny the younger recounts a marvellous tale of the acknowledgement of corruption in a letter in which he turns to discussing a staunch champion of public probity, Junius Mauricus. Mauricus was dining with Nerva (emperor AD 96-98) at a small party, where Fabricius Veiento was also present. This Veiento was a notorious crook, with a special line in taking bribes to fix promotions in government, and Pliny comments 'I need do no more than name the creature'. But the emperor Nerva seemed to be on very pally terms with him indeed ('even leaning on his shoulder', says Pliny). The conversation then turned to another notorious degenerate, the blind Catullus Messalinus, 'whose loss of sight had increased his cruelty, so that he knew neither fear, shame, nor pity, and consequently was often used [by the previous emperor] to aim at honest men like a weapon which flies blindly and unthinkingly to its mark. Everyone at table was talking freely about his murderous activities when the emperor asked "I wonder what would have happened to him were he alive today?" "He would be dining with us," Mauricus replied.'

Crunch.

THE MIDDLE WAY

Extremes of wealth, poverty or corruption make good subjects for historians because they are easy to discern. The man in the middle is often less easy to pick out, even during election times when 'middle England' is supposed to hold the key. Aristotle defined 'middle Greeks' broadly in terms of their wealth and desires, and saw them as a positive force for good.

Wedded to his doctrine of the 'mean' (i.e. that extremes should be avoided and the middle way was best), Aristotle reckoned that the best form of constitution was one in which 'middle people', as he calls them, were dominant. Such people, being neither excessively rich nor excessively poor, avoided the vices of the wealthy (contempt for others and refusal to be ruled), and of the impoverished (envy and a servile mentality). Again, since they did not covet the possessions of others, as the poor did, and the rich did not covet theirs, they were secure.

Next, middle people were least reluctant to hold office, but also least eager to: Aristotle thought that both excessive desire for and excessive hostility to public service were 'detrimental to states'. Most important of all, a middling condition was one most people could aspire to: after all, 'the state aims to consist as far as possible of those who are like and equal, a condition found chiefly among the middle people'.

A state divided into two – which for Aristotle meant the poor and the rich – could never be at peace, because the differences would constantly set the two sides against each other. What was required was a state with a large middle ground – both for its own intrinsic virtue, and to defuse extremists on either flank. Only in this way could a state be secure, and free from division and faction.

So any politician who proposed extremes, e.g. that unlimited personal wealth creation was to be encouraged, would have struck Aristotle as dangerous. Aristotle was equally suspicious of any ideology which set its manifesto out in terms of supporting one section of society against another (he thought this was the problem with democracy, though he was not opposed in principle to collective decision-making). So, for example, he exhorted oligarchies to cultivate the poor and democracies the rich. Again, since Aristotle did not believe that people were naturally equal, he could not see why they should be treated equally: so what kind of superiority should qualify a person for power? Certainly not the random votes of citizens: power was far too important a prerogative for that. Good birth, ownership of property, and moral qualities like justice and courage were priorities. But even worse for our present incumbents, Aristotle believed that the purpose of the state was to enable its citizens to live *well*, which he defined not in terms of economics but of culture. A leader who did not himself live up to the highest standards of education and culture could not by definition develop a state in the required way.

Aristotle hinted that he favoured enlightened tyrants, but in their absence looked for a balance between oligarchy and democracy. He could well have approved of our system of elective oligarchy, if not of our leaders.

Naming and shaming

If Aristotle was keen on avoiding extremes, it was because ancient Greeks went to them so often. Being seen to be independent and your own master, at whatever cost, was as important as coming out on top (see p. 144). But like a squash ladder, for those on top the more people there are below, and therefore the more there are who want to displace you and the more enemies you risk making. Greeks were well aware of who their friends were (people with whom they made common cause) and who their enemies, and knew the risks of shedding friends the higher they rose.

It was a commonplace of Greek ethics to 'do good to your friends and harm to your enemies' – the ethics of the soccer pitch. It was the soccer pitch in another sense too – you performed under the public gaze. It was public evaluation, not your own personal assessment, of your performance that counted. These are not the terms in which we are encouraged to describe and account for our actions today. As a result we have developed transparent absurdities like self-assessment – absurd because you can never prove them wrong except by others' assessment, so you may as well not have bothered in the first place (put 'absolutely brilliant' on all your self-assessment forms and see what happens). But that's education for you. Hence the outrage at the 'naming and shaming' policy directed at failing schools.

Aidôs, the ancient Greek word for 'a sense of shame', covered a wide range of feelings, including awe, fear (particularly of punishment) and respect. It was generated by acting below one's best, in front of friends or gods. For example, Homeric heroes urge on their men to stand firm in battle, or reproach them in retreat, by saying 'Put *aidôs* in your hearts'. They urge on themselves in precisely the same way. When in Homer's *Iliad* the Trojan hero Hector is standing outside the gates of Troy awaiting Achilles' attack, he admits he should have taken earlier advice to lead a retreat back into the city. As it is, he says to himself, 'I have destroyed my people by my rash actions, and now feel *aidôs* in front of the Trojan men and women in case someone more cowardly than I shall say of me "Hector, trusting in his strength, destroyed his people".' So he concludes that the only thing to do now is fight, and either kill Achilles and return, or be killed by him in front of the city and win renown by a noble death.

The point is that, without *aidôs*, there could be no honour. Unless a hero was able to judge what others considered shameful, he could not expect the status or high valuation in other people's eyes that he craved. That he was so able to judge indicates that there was broad agreement about what constituted honourable and shameful behaviour. But we have lost the taste for such judgements these days, which is why the 'name and shame' policy has been dropped.

The honours system

The ancient Greek word usually translated 'honour', *timê*, meant at root 'valuation'. They, like us, had an honours system, which was very important to them. To be honoured, you had to benefit the city, usually through massive public endowments. The city would then put up a monument to you, inscribing your good deeds. Though in fifth-century Athens this practice was rejected as hostile to democratic ideals, by the second century AD Athenians were so keen to give new honours that they even took old monuments and re-inscribed them, to the fury of the displaced families.

The important difference between the Greek system and ours is that in Athens, decisions about honours were debated and taken in *public*, at the people's Assembly. In so fiercely a competitive a society, envy and resentment over the results were inevitable. Such tensions were dealt with partly by the counter-rhetoric of 'moderation' and 'nothing in excess', partly by the parallel Greek dishonours system and the rhetoric of revenge.

The arena for this was also the Assembly and the law-courts, where

Greeks looked for ways in which to turn personal grievances into actionable issues. So in Greek political trials or impeachments the argument was often not whether X was guilty, but what the people should do about him, now that he was before them, whether guilty or not (President Clinton must know the feeling: cf. p. 76). Financial ruin, loss of *timê* (here in its technical sense of 'citizen rights'), exile or even death were what the aggrieved party hoped to inflict. Nor was there any need to disguise motive: one Greek court-case began with the prosecutor openly declaring that his purpose in bringing the case was to get revenge on the defendant.

Seeing Great Men Brought Low was as much of a thrill then as it is now – more so, probably, because people then were so acutely status-conscious and we are supposed to have grown out of this affectation. One certain way of riding for a fall in the Greek world was to act in such a way that people thought you guilty of *hybris* (see p. 149). This to an ancient Greek meant something much nastier and more interesting than 'pride'. It meant 'behaviour calculated to degrade and humiliate others' – depriving them of their status, in other words. This unexpressed desire is never far from the surface where power is at stake and one has opponents to deal with. We are politer about it these days, but the desire to avenge and humiliate has not gone away.

The Athenian comic playwright Aristophanes knew all about it. His comedies laid into politicians with a gusto which would have horrified those who feel we do not show due 'respect' for our politicians. When the great statesman Pericles died in 429 BC, his place was taken by Cleon, and Aristophanes (like the fifth-century BC historian Thucydides) did not approve. Aristophanes opens his comedy *Knights* (424 BC) with two slaves discovering an oracle that Cleon will be removed from power by someone even more uneducated and vulgar than himself – a tripe-seller. Enter a tripe-seller, who is at once pounced on and told his destiny. He is doubtful about his abilities and qualifications, but the slaves reassure him that the fewer he has, the better:

> *T-S*: But I am unworvy to 'old great power.
> *Slave*: What d'you mean, 'unworvy'? Not got any secret virtues on your conscience, have you? I mean, you're not a toff, are you?
> *T-S*: Blimey, no! Scum of the earth, me.
> *Slave*: Phew! Best thing that can happen to anyone who wants a future in politics.

T-S: But 'ang on. I 'ardly bin to school. Not a GCSE in sight. Well, I can just abaht read and write.

Slave: Pity, that – much better if you couldn't at all. Look here, you don't think politics is for the educated these days, or anyone of good character, do you? No, it's for illiterate oafs like you!

Naturally, when Cleon and the tripe-seller compete for the favour of the people, Cleon is outdone for vulgarity at every turn by his revolting opponent. Among much else, he is accused of being non-Athenian, sexually deviant and a menial trader – terrible slurs for proud Athenians.

Cleon, in fact, was politically no slouch. That made no more difference to Aristophanes than it would to satirists today. A target is there to be hit.

TAX ATTACKS

Every year newspapers titillate the envy of their readers by telling them who are the 300 richest people in the UK. Ancient Athenians would have been very interested indeed.

Income tax was invented by William Pitt the younger in 1799 as a temporary measure to finance the war effort against Napoleon. It has been with us virtually ever since. Greeks did not tax income (which would usually be agricultural produce anyway), but property, in two ways. An irregular tax was levied during emergencies, i.e. (as with Pitt) war. It was imposed only on a selected few, the six thousand wealthiest Athenians. It could represent as little as 0.25% of taxable capital, but was prestigious enough (and rare enough) for those who paid it to boast about it.

The only regular tax in Athens was that levied on the property of the very richest, to fund specific annual services: in particular, the great dramatic festivals (in January and April every year when tragedies and comedies were staged in open competition with each other) and the equipping and manning of the triremes which brought Athens its power and empire in the fifth century BC. This state duty was called a *leitourgia* (origin of our 'liturgy'), and those liable for it were usually men with property worth *c.* 4 talents or more (= 24,000 drachmas – a skilled workman was paid about 350 drs. a year).

For many Athenians, this duty was a great honour. Costing anything from 50 to over 5,000 drs., it publicly confirmed status and importance, and we have records of Athenians who, though failing to qualify, actually volunteered to carry out a *leitourgia*. (It was freely admitted that if done well it could bring considerable political or personal advancement.) Others tried to avoid it. If someone (let us call him A) appointed to carry out the duty thought someone else (B) was richer, A could challenge B to a property exchange. If B agreed, property was exchanged and A carried out the duty; if B refused – and the only reason can have been that B knew he really was richer – B carried out the duty.

The virtue of the system was that status-mad Athenians were not going to allow any public service to which their name was personally attached to be anything but the very best. Our government could do worse than commit the wealthiest not to give their money to the state, but to take named responsibility for certain state-funded projects instead. Can one envisage a Marks and Spencer Motorway being permanently dug up for repairs during the long summer months? But perhaps Virgin railways are not a good advertisement for the scheme.

It is the psychology of this that is so appealing. The liturgist knows what he is giving money to ('hypothecation' of taxes – a good Greek word), and it enhances his status. What might have been seen as a brutal compulsory tax has come to seem more like voluntary benefaction. The government would do well to develop this 'benefactor' mentality. If it wants more money, let it identify x worthwhile projects, and invite y million liturgists each to pay £z. It should then instruct them to support whichever of the projects they like – the element of choice is vital – with the promise that their help will, if they so desire, be publicly acknowledged.

With this sort of scheme in mind, it was a pity the Queen did not consult an ancient historian when she recently agreed to pay income tax for the first time. She could have done an Augustus. In 'My Achievements' (his own account of his reign) Augustus (first emperor of Rome, 31 BC – AD 14) boasts about the amount of his own money he had personally spent for the benefit of the Roman people – public buildings, banquets, free bread, extravagant games, cheap baths (etc.). So Her Majesty was ill-advised to pour income tax into the undiscriminating maw of the taxman, who will fritter it away on nothing in particular. She should instead have agreed to finance out of her own purse a series of named public endowments of her choice. Open classes in Latin and ancient Greek up and down the country would command widespread popular support, but doubtless there are other equally deserving causes one could think of.

Privataxation

The Romans, with a vast empire to run and exploit, developed wide-ranging tax-collecting regimes. They even privatised tax-collection. This scheme was invented by Gaius Gracchus in 123 BC. It seems that he legislated for the right to collect taxes in the new and wealthy Roman province of Asia (in modern Turkey) to be auctioned off to the highest bidder. The winning consortium would pay off the provincials' tax debt for the year, and keep everything they collected. These tax-collectors were called *publicani* (the hated 'publicans' of the New Testament) and a very lucrative business it was.

There were two advantages to the system. First, it continued Roman policy of utilising private individuals in order to avoid creating a professional body of financial officers. More important, it meant the government got its taxes for the year from the winning consortium all at one go, at the beginning of the fiscal year, without spending time, money and effort on collection. True, government probably accepted a price lower than the total theoretical sum to be collected (otherwise the collectors would make no profit), but the advantages easily outweighed this loss.

Inevitably the system was abused by ruthless collectors working hand-in-glove with corrupt provincial governors and officials. In a letter to his brother Quintus (60 BC), who was serving as governor of Asia at the time, Cicero comments on the difficulty of keeping the collectors happy while preventing them bleeding the provincials white. The first Roman emperor Augustus (31 BC – AD 14) tried to control abuses, but they continued: under Nero (in AD 55) it was even suggested that the only way to end them was to abolish the taxes completely.

Privatised tax-collection and the chance to pick your own taxman are surely vote winners. If government cannot steel itself to levy income tax this way, it should at least urge local councils to experiment on these lines.

Tax benefits

At least the Romans knew all about keeping their own people happy, unlike our own much-loved Chancellors with their grindingly tedious annual budgets and joke predictions of 'growth'. The modern office worker enjoys about 130 free days a year. The Romans had anything from 57 to 177, finally settling for 135. At these times state-funded public shows were put on as a feature of state religion, often celebrating some great triumph or escape from disaster. Drama, musicals and cabaret, especially mimes, were the staple diet. But on the last day there was the chariot-racing. Romans, including many emperors, were wild about it (we read of one fan immolating himself at the funeral of the charioteer Felix in 77 BC), and crowd control was strict (fans could be banned or fined for bad behaviour).

Tax-exemptions were another way the Romans raised people's spirits, especially in the empire. Whole communities could be granted exemption as a reward for favours, as Greece was by Nero in AD 67. Individuals and special groups could also be targeted. Under the empire, cities were even allowed to exempt a fixed number of doctors, teachers and lecturers from taxes, as long as their work remained up to the mark – a much better idea than all this 'extra pay for excellence' which so infuriates today's unions. If the government cannot afford to pay for nation-wide public shows, it should at least do the next best thing and lay on some TV spectaculars – it might even raise revenue through them (cf. p. 93). As for tax-exemptions, they could be used to encourage a whole range of government-approved behaviour, from continual wearing of seat-belts, nicotine patches and condoms (all at once gets a bonus) to paying your taxes on time.

CALL TO ARMS

Winston Churchill, we are told, could and should have made peace with Hitler in 1940. When Philip, king of Macedon 359-336 BC, was planning to subdue Greece, it was Demosthenes in Athens who urged the Greek city states to stand up to the tyrant. They eventually did, but it was too late, and in 338 BC Philip defeated the Greek coalition at the battle of Chaeronea.

In 330 BC Demosthenes was asked by his political opponent Aeschines to defend his policy of resistance. Demosthenes agrees that his policy had failed, and continues:

But if Athens, which had thought it right to lead the rest of Greece in this matter, had then abandoned its responsibilities, she would have been held guilty of betraying Greece to Philip. If, without striking a blow, she had abandoned the cause from which, however perilous, our forefathers had never flinched, is there a man here now who would not have spat in your face? How could we have looked visitors to our city straight in the eye,

Government-approved behaviour

if the result had been what it is – Philip, lord and master of all Greece – and if other nations had fought gallantly to avert that calamity, but we had not lifted a finger? How many of our ancient enemies would not willingly and gratefully have granted Athens permission to keep what she had and to take what she chose – if only she would abandon her leadership and obey others' orders?

The Athenians of old thought of themselves as men born not to a father and mother, but to a country. What is the difference? The man who considers that he is born only to his parents awaits his natural and destined end. The son of his country is willing to die rather than see her enslaved, and will look on the outrages and indignities visited on a nation in subjection as more terrible than death itself.

The Romans would have agreed with Demosthenes' stance. They endlessly debated the pros and cons of 'honourable' as opposed to 'self-interested' behaviour and usually plumped for the former because as well as being glorious, it invariably turned out to be *more* in one's interest than the purely selfish option. History reinforced the message.

Honour in war

The Romans under Camillus were engaged in a lengthy siege of Falerii *c.* 390 BC. A treacherous Falerian schoolmaster, however, who still regularly exercised his boys outside the walls, saw his opportunity and led his charges right into the Roman camp. Since the children were all the sons of Falerii's great and good, the schoolmaster announced to the Romans and Camillus that Falerii was now at the Romans' mercy.

The reply that the Roman historian Livy puts into Camillus' mouth is instructive. He rejects the schoolmaster's values, calling him an unprincipled swine; Rome and Falerii may have no political ties, but 'we are bound together none the less, and always shall be, by the bonds of common humanity'. There are laws of war as well as of peace: further, 'we have drawn our swords not against children, but against men, armed like ourselves'. The schoolmaster has tried to bring Falerii down by a vile act, without precedent, but Camillus will bring it down by the traditional Roman arts – 'courage, persistence and arms'.

Camillus has the traitor stripped and bound, gives the boys sticks, and tells them to beat him back into Falerii. The Falerians, moved by

Roman honour and Camillus' justice, at once give in to their besiegers. In their submission to the Roman Senate, they say 'From this war, two things have emerged which the world would do well to take to heart. You preferred honour to an easy victory. We now recognise your sway.' Winning wars is a matter of winning minds. Dropping bombs is the easy part.

Inhuman nature

The greatest historian of war, the Athenian Thucydides, hoped that his history of the war between Athens and Sparta (431-404 BC) would be a 'possession for ever'. His analysis of the dynamics of power does not lose its force with the passage of time.

A flash-point of the Athens-Sparta conflict was the attack of Thebes (allied to Sparta) on its close neighbour and age-old rival Plataea. After a bloody four-year siege the Plataeans were offered a 'fair trial' in return for voluntary submission. Having no option, they accepted and found the 'trial' consisted of a single question: 'Have you done anything to help Sparta in the present war?'

As the Plataeans pointed out, if the Spartans were Plataea's enemies, the Spartans could hardly complain at receiving no help; but if the Spartans expected Plataeans to help them because they were Plataea's friends, why had they attacked the Plataeans in the first place? Anyway, the Plataeans based their appeal for mercy on past heroics, the history of their dealings with Sparta and Thebes, and the injustice of the present 'trial'. This appeal was cynically answered by Sparta's allies, the revenge-hungry Thebans, that only evil deeds needed long statements, to disguise them. 'If everyone, like the Spartans, asked a single question in such cases, there would be fewer efforts to cover up wrongdoing.' The Spartans were implacable. Two hundred Plataeans stood 'trial' and were executed. Thucydides' comment is telling: 'It was because of the Thebans that the Spartans treated the Plataeans so mercilessly: they considered that at this stage, the Thebans were useful to them.'

It is all here: the especial ruthlessness of *neighbours* engaged in conflict; the pointless destruction of small communities in 'greater' causes; treachery in the guise of justice; hatred posing as champion of what is right; the irrelevance of past behaviour, except for past wrongs; and the subservience of all considerations of mercy or morality to the imperative of revenge. Thucydides expressed the hope that men would learn from his history. We are slow learners.

The language of war

Thucydides saw the corrupting effect of the rhetoric of war, preventing people seeing the issues for what they were. His account of revolution in Corfu in 427 BC is still the best commentary on this phenomenon. Athens and Sparta had declared war in 431 BC and set about winning other Greek cities to their cause. The two factions in Corfu were the first actually to fight over the issue, with appalling and indiscriminate slaughter.

Thucydides then describes with horror how revolution spread from city to city. Words, he said, changed their meaning. Mindless aggression became the courage you would expect in a comrade. Moderation disguised weakness: fanaticism was the mark of the real man. Violent opinions could always be trusted, and anyone who objected to them was suspect. Revenge was more important even than self-preservation, while pacts were made merely to overcome temporary difficulties. A victory won by treachery was a mark of intelligence. Neither justice nor the interests of the people prevented men doing anything to win power by any means, and those who relied on policy rather than naked force were easily destroyed. Conscience was ignored: more attention was given to the man who could justify outrages attractively.

Thucydides ends: 'In exacting revenge on others, men take it upon themselves to begin the process of repealing those general laws of humanity which are there to give hope to all who are in distress, instead of remembering that there may come a time when they, too, will need their protection.' But such behaviour is universal, 'human nature being what it is, though there may be different degrees of savagery and the general rules will vary as the circumstances change'.

Law and peace

As for peace, various instructive elements went into the construction of an ancient peace-treaty. Decisions had to be taken about, for example, the length of time during which the treaty was to be in force; a possible hand-over of prisoners, land, and material goods; an exchange of hostages, whose number, length of detention and social status were all carefully determined beforehand (the point being that the lower the social status of the hostages, the less concern there was over breaking the treaty); the erection of pillars in public places, usually sanctuaries, with the terms inscribed on them; and the form of oath with which the treaty was sealed (including such formulae as 'I shall abide by the terms of this treaty honestly and sincerely').

The point that lay at the very heart of an ancient Greek peace-treaty was the principle of *summachia* – 'fighting together', an agreement to wage war against anyone who attacked any of the treaty's signatories. Thus when Sparta and Athens agreed terms in 421 BC, 'in case of enemy invasion of or hostile action against Sparta, Athens will come to their aid ...' and *vice versa*. Another ancient treaty puts the agreement even more sharply: 'having the same friends and enemies' as each other.

This applies with especial force, for example, to the recent agreement over Ireland. It is all very well to say that it is Catholic/Protestant attitudes that count and it will take generations for these to change. Athenians and Spartans were not exactly bosom pals, but, like all Greeks, they saw that *summachia* was an essential component of any peace-treaty (though it did not guarantee that treaties lasted their full term). Only when all parties to the Stormont talks agree that they will all support each other against mutual enemies and act upon their word will a secure peace emerge.

PEERLESS PROPOSALS

If the papers are not banging on about 'the need for constitutional change' (as if we had a constitution), they are wringing their hands about the state of the monarchy and the need for it to 'move with the times'. This is quite the wrong way to change our mighty organs of state.

Like us, the Romans had no constitution and, like us, they loved it. They looked back fondly to the days of 509 BC when the little city of Rome expelled the king (Tarquin) imposed on it by its powerful Etruscan neighbours to the north and the republic sprang into life. They rejoiced that their institutions continued to develop through experiment and modification. The elder Cato (234-149 BC) boasted that it was the strength of the Roman 'constitution' to have been put in place not at one moment by one man but over a period of centuries.

But when this highly effective republican system began to crumble in the first century BC as dynasts Caesar and Pompey, with armies at their back, rode rough shod over rule by the Senate and the traditional ways of doing things, Romans changed their tune. They looked back to an idealised, unchanging past, stable and secure. Julius Caesar, the upstart 'king', was assassinated on the Ides (fifteenth) of March 44 BC to restore this fiction.

But the world had changed, irrevocably. Thirteen years after Caesar's death, his adopted son and heir Octavian became the first Roman emperor, Augustus. He achieved this momentous transition partly with the help of a very simple message – no change. The old Republic had been restored. Its officers and Senate remained intact. No need, therefore, to panic. It was back to the good old days.

Our world, too, is changing, irrevocably. Those who scream for change will find it happening more easily and smoothly if they announce that (thank heavens) no change is taking place. Nevertheless, since violent change is proposed, however unwisely, for the House of Lords, there is a strong case for daring experiment. It is called democracy. It has not been tried for some 2,400 years.

Greek Lords

The House of Lords should be turned into a version of the Athenian Council (*boulê* – see p. 72). This Council was a standing committee, a portion of it on duty twenty-four hours a day, ready to receive and if necessary debate any political issue drawn to its attention. It consisted of 500 Athenian citizens over 30, each with a deputy in case of illness, appointed by a combination of local election and national lot, in a number proportionate to the size of the local constituencies. The 500 served for one year only. No one could serve more than twice in all.

The function of the Council was to serve the people's Assembly. This Assembly (consisting of all male citizens over 18) was Athens' sovereign body. It met every nine days to debate and take all decisions that government takes nowadays, and the Council served it broadly in two ways. It drew up the agenda and terms of debate for the Assembly meetings (and summoned it in emergencies) and then ensured the Assembly's decisions were put into effect.

One cannot quite imagine the New House of Lords serving the Commons in this way, but it is the Athenian principle of appointment that is so appealing. Let the New House of Lords do what the Lords currently does, i.e. review Commons business. But let it consist of any members of the public over 30 prepared to serve in it, appointed regionally, in proportion, by election-with-lot, with a deputy. Let the allotted members serve for (say) three years and no more, with elections on a rolling system so that there is a yearly turnover. For the first time in our history, this would introduce an element of democracy into our oligarchic system. It would break the stultifying grip of party control in one area of political life. It would educate the citizen body and make its voice heard. Since the Lords have no authority over the Commons anyway, at worst it would do no harm.

This principle of appointment is a sound one for anyone willing to engage in public service on public committees of whatever kind. For example, the general public is always being invited to put itself forward to serve on quangos – those 'quasi-autonomous non-governmental organisations' whose currently unelected members spend so much public money on our behalf (e.g. NHS Trusts). Those keen for appointment could put themselves forward for election at local level (after a due *dokimasia* – see p. 75), and those elected put in a hat for the final selection by lot. True, those wishing to serve would be alerted to the fact that their performance in office would be monitored and incompetence punished, on the Athenian system. But that never stopped Athenians (see p. 75).

Roman Lords

On the other hand, if the principle of 'collective experience' that the House of Lords enshrines is a valuable quality, let the Roman Senate provide the model for the new House of Lords and put the Commons very firmly in their place (see p. 80). The Roman republican constitution had three elements: annually elected executives who did the work ('magistrates'); a Senate; and the electors, i.e. the people of Rome. Magistrates had to work their way up step by step. First they sought election as quaestor (minimum age 30: i/c finance); then aedile (city works and price control); praetor (40: law and military); and finally the big one, consul (42: head of state, chairman of Senate, military commander), of whom there were always (cunningly) two.

The Senate (cf. *senex*, 'old man') was a permanent standing body, consisting of all magistrates, past and present, charged with overseeing all state business. Election as quaestor qualified one for membership of the Senate for life. Though strictly advisory, the Senate possessed such weight of authority and experience that it effectively controlled policy.

The people elected all magistrates and also approved all new legislation before it could become law (even in oligarchic Rome, in other words, the people had far more power than we do). They also elected 'people's tribunes' to the Senate to protect their own interests: these had rights of veto over all legislation in case the aristocrats on the Senate cut up rough.

So: sack all MPs and turn the Lords into the Senate. Let the people elect executive officers in the shape of magistrates (sacked MPs, if they offer themselves) every year to do state business (chairing select committees in co-operation with the Senate and civil servants); let all new legislation be agreed in Senate and then by the people; let People's tribunes be elected to veto legislation; and let two consuls, please, be appointed from *different* parties.

ROYAL ROAD

Now that reports of royal cavortings have died down, there may be no need to call on the experience of the first Roman emperor Augustus (31 BC – AD 14). He had a brisk way with members of his own household who strayed out of line, not to mention those who encouraged them.

The first century BC in Rome saw something of a sexual revolution, when married women of noble birth openly flaunted their adulterous liaisons (like Lesbia, probably Clodia, wife of Metellus [consul, 60 BC], with the poet Catullus). Augustus, perceiving such behaviour as a threat to the political and social order, introduced legislation intended both to curb adultery and to encourage marriage and the production of legitimate children among the ruling classes (see p. 67). It was a failure (and Augustus himself was not exactly innocent), but this did not stop him taking a severe line with his daughter Julia. If the stories are true, she was a practical joker, born to have 'fun', enjoying riotous parties and assignations with her many lovers in the very middle of the Forum. So in 2 BC Augustus banished her to Pandateria, a minute island west of Naples (modern Ventotene), having exiled her lover Gracchus to Kerkenna (an island east of Tunisia). In AD 8, the same treatment was meted out to the poet Ovid. His deliciously immoral poem *Ars Amatoria* ('Seduction Made Easy') did not find favour with Augustus but inevitably enjoyed great success after the Julia scandal, and Ovid also seems to have had some liaison with Augustus' grand-daughter, another Julia of inclinations similar to her mother's. Augustus exiled him to Tomis (Constanta) in Romania on the Black Sea, whence he wrote a stream of whinging letters home, and her to Tremiti (Adriatic isles off central Italy).

This was the standard punishment. The mildest form of exile was temporary expulsion from Roman territory; the harshest, banishment in perpetuity to a specific location ('an island or oasis', as the saying went), with loss of property and citizenship, and death for returning. But exile was also available *voluntarily* to any Roman threatened with capital proceedings, and even those on whom the death sentence had already been passed were usually given time to flee before it was carried out. Her Majesty could bear all this in mind for the next royal generation.

Right rite

The government has forced Buckingham Palace to take steps to cut down the ritual associated with the State Opening of Parliament. But how can you curtail ritual? The whole point of ritual (*ritus*, derivation unknown) is that it is a symbolic routine, performed in a set sequence, at a set time and place, hallowed by observance, usage and custom. Any omission, deviation or indeed hesitation is a matter of concern. Repetition is all. To change it is to destroy it, and therefore to invalidate its high purpose, calling forth who knows what retribution from the mysterious powers whose good will it is designed to solicit?

Ritual accompanied all the great social and religious occasions of the ancient world. It usually involved extravagant dressing up (in fifteenth-century BC Minoan Crete, ritual is shown being performed by dog-like monsters with snouts, pointed ears and paws). After the event it was common for a committee to check that the ceremony had been properly conducted. There was a terrible flap on one occasion, for example, when, after a great ceremony in honour of the god Dionysus in Athens, it was discovered that a key female participant was not Athenian born and bred. Again, a sacrifice was not deemed valid if anything ill-omened happened: let the bull stumble (i.e. not go willingly), let a cry break out at the wrong moment, let the liver resemble a hob-nailed boot, and the whole ceremony would have to be conducted again. The Greek general Xenophon was held up for days during his famous march back from Babylon to Greece (and even feared running out of bulls) when the priests encountered a nasty run of unprepossessing livers. Both the Athenian Assembly and the Roman congregations could be called to a halt if something untoward interrupted routine (it was not uncommon for meetings thus to be abandoned for nefarious political purposes).

So it bodes ill for parliament that ancient ritual is being cast aside and that those hallowed ceremonial figures – Bluemantle Pursuivant, Silver Stick in Waiting, all dressed (and probably named) rather like those monsters of ancient Minoan cult – will vanish from the procession. At least the Great Officers of State have had the sense to insist on continuing to walk backwards ahead of the Sovereign. They at any rate will be saved.

There was even a recent proposal to move Her Majesty out of

Buckingham Palace into a new, more modest home, saving money and reflecting all that is 'best' in modern British taste and design. At least there is nothing new in that. The Flavian emperors of Rome (AD 69-96) had much the same idea. Before them, emperors from Augustus to Nero had built on a huge and extravagant scale. Nero, indeed, was said to have set fire to the city in AD 64 in order to create the space for his vast new palace the *Domus Aurea* ('Golden House'). This fire destroyed virtually all existing monuments of historical importance, and Nero set about rebuilding with a Fire Relief Fund. The resulting *Domus Aurea* extended to nearly two hundred acres, was covered in gold and jewels, featured a huge octagonal rotating dining room, a forty-seater loo, ornamental ponds, fountains and wild animals, and was fronted by a 120' high statue of himself.

The Flavians, affecting to regard this 'corruption' with distaste, started to knock it down. Vespasian, proclaiming his humble origins and modest desire to serve the people alone, built the Colosseum over Nero's ornamental ponds. Titus built his Baths over the very centre of the *Domus Aurea*. Domitian completed their work with a brand new palace and various other public works (paid for, interestingly, by cutting back the military). The result of all this was, of course, building on a far vaster scale than Nero could ever have envisaged, and at far greater expense. It will be cheaper to leave Buckingham Palace alone.

5

Schools for Scandal?

Greek archaeologists have found Aristotle's Lyceum (Latinised spelling of Greek *Lukeion*, so called because it was built in a sanctuary to *Apollon Lukeios*, 'Apollo of the wolf', one of Apollo's many epithets, cf. French *lycée*).

The Lyceum had been a popular public meeting place long before Aristotle became associated with it. Education and pederastic culture were closely connected in ancient Athens (see p. 130) and the gymnasium at the Lyceum, where young men trained naked, attracted older men. Famous intellectuals gave lectures there. Socrates frequented it regularly. The number of places for a walk (*peripatos*) in the area gave the name 'peripatetic' to the type of philosophy Aristotle practised there.

Aristotle, born in 384 BC in Stagira (northern Greece), studied under Plato at his Academy in Athens for twenty years and was tutor to Alexander the Great (see p. 42) for seven before founding his 'school' at the Lyceum in 335 BC. It is wrong to think of such a place as a sort of modern university. Aristotle did not think of research and education in terms of market-share, counselling procedures for the mentally deficient or modules leading to 'skills' relevant to the 'world of work' (he was remarkably backward in this respect). He lectured, we are told, to chosen pupils in the morning and to the general public at night (the first adult evening classes). Indeed he took the view that you knew your subject only if you could teach it.

Lecture techniques

One would love to know what it was like to attend one of his lectures. Slightly chaotic, perhaps, if (as many scholars argue) the rather disorganised structure of argument in a number of his works suggests that they survive only in lecture-note form. Students would certainly have had to work harder than those Plutarch was acquainted with. His advice on listening to lectures clearly comes from bitter experience.

Generally, Plutarch advises students to sit up straight with no lounging or sprawling, and look directly at the speaker with an attitude of keen, undivided attention. Frowning, sour looks, roving glances, writhing about, crossing the legs, nodding, whispering, sleepy yawns and letting the head drop are all to be avoided. Three types of listener attract Plutarch's particular censure. The envious man will pay no attention to what is being said, so busy is he checking the reactions of the rest of the audience for signs of discontent and disapproval. The excessively enthusiastic also do themselves no favours, because they are uncritically susceptible to wonderful displays of verbal fireworks, which do nothing but entertain. Once the pleasure of hearing them has passed, nothing remains, so one must be a keen and ruthless critic of content. Then there are those tiresome listeners who, 'full of presumption and ingrained self-importance', sit there looking wise and profound, determined not to be moved by anything.

Questions at the end also need attention. Plutarch is as severe on modest people who cannot bring themselves to ask questions at the time and then much later 'trouble lecturers with questions they should have asked earlier, trying to catch up' as he is on the lazy, who repeatedly ask questions about the same thing, and the know-alls who, 'keen to be thought astute and attentive, exhaust the speaker with their verbosity and officiousness by continually raising inessential matters of no importance'. Most important of all, Plutarch suggests asking the speaker only those questions that he is fitted to answer: no point in trying to 'split wood with a key or open the door with an axe', as he puts it.

For Plutarch, a lecture was not one-way traffic. As guests at dinner parties have duties to hosts, as (in another striking image) a catcher in a ball game has to respond to the thrower, so, he argues, there must be a certain accord between speaker and hearer, an awareness of mutual obligations. All this will strike modern students, naturally, as outrageous.

Perhaps Aristotle had better experiences. But for one so out of tune with modern educational thought and so lamentably ignorant of the importance of research and teaching assessment procedures, he really did surprisingly well, single-handedly laying the foundations for almost the whole of European thought in areas such as science, philosophy, history, theology, poetry and drama.

Sun-tan teaching

Plato would not have approved. He would have approved even less of education today, when even more students at even more universities are being taught in even larger classes. Plato wrote his books on philosophy in the form of dialogues because, unlike Aristotle, he mistrusted books and lectures (Plato actually invented the dialogue form). Since true education depended on the interaction of minds, dialogue was at the centre of it. His books therefore were an attempt to reproduce that experience for the reader.

Plato devised a method for determining whether anyone was serious about education when in 361 BC he was reluctantly persuaded to attempt (for a second time) to turn Dionysius II, tyrant of Syracuse, into a philosopher-king of the sort he was convinced could alone cure the troubles of mankind. In his famous 'Seventh Letter', Plato describes the test he invented which was calculated not to compromise the dignity of the learner, 'especially one as full of second-hand ideas as Dionysius'.

Briefly, it consisted of revealing to the pupil 'the nature of the subject as a whole, and all the stages that must be gone through, and how much labour is required'. Those who were captivated with the 'divine spark' for learning and believed that life could be lived in no other way would find it 'so wonderful that they will pursue it with all their might if life is to be worth living'. They would pressurise themselves and their tutors till either they reached their goal or could make their own way without help. Plato likens the search for truth to a flame being kindled by a leaping spark, and says this comes only after a long partnership in a common life devoted to that search.

His test, he argued, 'has the advantage that a man has only himself to blame if he cannot meet the demands of the subject, and his guide is absolved from responsibility'. As for those who had no aptitude or interest, for whom learning was little more than 'a superficial veneer, like men developing a sun-tan', once they saw 'how much there is to learn and the labour involved and the disciplined way of life the subject requires', they would quickly abandon it. It is a very simple and effective test. That is why no university dare implement it. Universities have no interest in determining who can benefit from education. They have become vast sun-beds, under government orders to ensure a general all-over tan.

Plato is making a vital distinction between active and passive learning. The one demands drive, energy and commitment, the other nothing but a flair for lying in the sun. Government policy that more and more people should 'be educated' (note the passive) and in increasingly massive classes suggests it adheres to the sun-tan theory of education. Students with a Platonic commitment to it have every right to be browned off (cf. p. 60).

Universities have become vast sun-beds

TEACHER KNOWS BEST

Plato, then, would have been amazed as, week after week, agony aunts pour out patronising advice to parents not to demand high standards of their children: they might 'alienate' the dears. Plato put this sort of reaction down to excessive democracy, which made people afraid of imposing or accepting authority. So 'teachers are afraid of their pupils and curry favour with them, while pupils despise their teachers ... the young turn any conversation or action into a trial of strength with their elders; meanwhile, older people adapt themselves to the younger ones, ooze frivolity and charm, and model their behaviour on the young'.

This was shocking to the ancients because (unlike today's parents) they firmly believed that adults knew better than their young. They did not regard children as fashion accessories or extensions of their own personalities (as we tend to), but as small adults, needing training to become proper adults and bring credit to their parents (what it was really all about). That meant teaching them reason, self-control and respect for experience.

Not that the ancients found child-rearing easy. The Roman public servant Pliny the younger, one of many, moaned about 'today's young': they 'know everything, respect no one, imitate no one, and set their own standards'. Plato, however, saw the key: he argues that rebuking and admonishing does no good 'these days'. What is required is *example*: if the old want the young to respect them and behave, they must respect the young and behave themselves. That is different from patronising them. It is not a difference our agony aunts seem able to understand.

Not more, but better

Plato would also have been amazed at the ends implicit in our system. Week by week, for example, we are told that industry needs more scientists and the workforce more graduates, 'if our exports are to compete with Japan/Germany/Korea/wherever'.

In his *Republic*, Plato sets out to describe an unrealisable ideal society where justice prevails. It contains three classes of people: workers (farmers, artisans, craftsmen, traders, sailors, etc.), who provide the economic basis of the society; soldiers, who protect it; and philosopher-kings, who rule it (the 'Guardians' – see pp. 11, 101). But how are these people to be put into the appropriate category? Plato is not precise, but does say that the categories of soldier and Guardian should be reserved for those with special qualities, which will need to be observed in the first place occurring naturally, and will then need to be developed by a programme of education. Only the very best will emerge as Guardians at the end of it – men and women demonstrating throughout their lives real 'intelligence and competence for the job, and care for the community'.

So if someone had said to Plato 'You need more Guardians', he would have thought him deranged. Plato's priority was excellence, not quantity. Strikingly, Plato applies this across the board: workers too must have special qualities, doing what comes best and most naturally to them.

Plato saw excellence and specialisation as connected. These days, when the world is changing so fast, specialisation may be a handicap. But one can never have enough of excellence. 'Different people are inherently suited for different activities', as Plato pointed out, and it is excellence in any skill or activity that is the priority. We do not need more scientists and graduates, but fewer – and much, much better.

Yes, minister

One thing, however, does not change: education ministers know best, their national curriculum is wonderful, and teachers are always to blame. In *Laws*, his blueprint for Utopia, Plato legislates that his Minister for Education will be over fifty and the father of legitimate sons and daughters. He will be the best all-round citizen in the state and hold office for five years. Since eternally valid truths exist and are known, he will not encourage freedom of inquiry and expression. He will simply tell the student what to learn, and when. There will be no escape. For example, Plato lays down three years for the study of literature and three for learning to play the lyre, and goes on 'neither the child nor its father must be allowed to extend or curtail these periods of study out of enthusiasm or distaste for the curriculum: that will be against the law'.

But what course book should determine what children should and should not learn? Why, Plato's *Laws*, of course. 'Teachers will be compelled to learn this material and speak well of it, and none should be employed who disapprove of it.'

So far, it is impossible to distinguish between Plato's *Laws* and our much-loved National Curriculum. The difference comes with enforcement. Here Plato makes the breakthrough which education ministers should emulate. If teachers and/or pupils are out of order, says Plato,

the responsibility for stopping them lies *with passers-by who witness it.*
If they fail to act, they should be held in the deepest disgrace and kept
under surveillance. This should be legislated for at once. Why blame
just teachers, unions, heads and governors if things go wrong, when
ministers can blame *everyone*?

Exam league tables would equally have struck chords with all
ancients. They loved competition, especially in education (see p. 144).
Schools did not exist so much as individual professors, to whom new
students attached themselves with extraordinary fanaticism. In late
Roman Athens, for example, students kept watch at the harbour
Piraeus to waylay incoming freshers. Since captains of these ships were
frequently paid by a professor to deliver their cargo to him and no one
else, landings would often take place at secret locations by night.
Libanius (AD 314-393), who was eventually to become a professor at
Antioch (in Syria), tells of the stories he heard as a youth about 'the
fighting between schools that took place in the heart of Athens: I had
heard of the cudgels, knives and stones they used, the wounds, the
court-actions, and the deeds of derring-do that students performed to
raise the prestige of their professors'; and he admits to looking forward
to joining in. When Libanius himself arrived at Athens, he was
promptly abducted by a group whose professor (Diophantus) he did
not wish to patronise. His captors locked him in a cell and kept him
there until he swore fidelity to Diophantus' school.

Naturally, when Libanius became a professor, he expounded on the
heroism of students who fought for their professor through thick and
thin, and complained about the lily-livered lot he now had: which of
them had ever courted danger or got into a fight on his behalf? The
more students a professor attracted, of course, the more money he
made. In today's brave new world of competition and payment by
numbers and results, these are important lessons for schools at the
bottom of the league, not to mention universities.

Reel education

But why is country-dancing not on the list of compulsory subjects? It
explains why Scottish education is so superior to English. In his
Republic, Plato discussed the sort of education which those who
wished to become the philosopher-kings in his ideal community would
have to undergo to become worthy of the honour. Since excellence of
character depended on excellence of experience, the first stage of education aimed to teach the young to recognise and respond to what was

noble, rhythmic, harmonious, and elegant. They therefore studied wholesome literature, music and gymnastics.

In the second stage, the student learned to look beyond the physical world to the absolute, unchanging reality behind it. So education was now devoted to mathematics – in particular, arithmetic, plane and solid geometry, astronomy and harmonics – and culminated in logic. Such studies began with the real world (counting troops, calculating land areas, examining the stars, etc.) but the ultimate aim was to show that by purely intellectual processes, eternally valid conclusions could be drawn. Mathematics, in other words, was a good model for showing that absolute truth was possible.

The basics of arithmetic and geometry, a sense of logic, harmony and rhythm, the value of elegance – what else is being inculcated in the Scots as they set and poussette their way to the music through their exquisitely structured reels and strathspeys in village hall or Perthshire country house? Hence their effortless superiority: they have been receiving a proper Platonic education from the moment they could walk.

They can also read and write. Research in Glasgow has shown that the old way of teaching to read – by the sounds letters make – is more effective than modern look-and-guess methods. 'Old' in this case is at least as old as St Jerome, who in AD 403 wrote a letter to Laeta, instructing her on how to teach her daughter Paula to read and write.

First of all, Laeta must have a set of ivory or boxwood letters made for Paula, and she must tell her their names. Paula must play with them, and learn their correct order 'by means of an easy song': but she must also mix them up and learn to recognise them without such artificial aid. So she will learn the alphabet, the names of the letters and their sounds.

Next, writing. Someone's hand should guide hers as she writes her first letters, or the outline of the letter should be drawn so that she can follow it. When it comes to putting syllables together to make words, she should be offered prizes for getting them right, and should work in company with friends, to stimulate competition. 'But she must not be scolded if she is rather slow: praise is the way to sharpen her wits.'

Above all, St Jerome warns, it is essential to make the lessons interesting, since 'a dislike engendered in childhood is likely to last into later years'. Nor must the teaching be haphazard, but directed towards a specific end. So Laeta must take care to choose appropriate words out of which Paula can construct her sentences, and St Jerome recommends 'the names of the prophets, apostles and the whole list of patriarchs from Adam downwards, as the gospels of St Matthew and St Luke give them'. One trembles to think who today's heroes might be.

Painful lessons

Despite St Jerome's ancient example, however, illiteracy is still a problem. One recent government tactic to solve it is the establishment of government-sponsored illiteracy summer schools. The younger Pliny had the idea some time ago, but it took a slightly different form.

The most useful thing to do in the summer hols, Pliny says to one Fuscus (pointing out that many have suggested it before) is to translate Greek into Latin and Latin into Greek. This kind of exercise, Pliny goes on, develops 'a precision and richness of vocabulary, a wide range of metaphor, a power of exposition, and, through imitation of the best models, a similar aptitude for original composition'. At the same time, he points out that 'anything which an ordinary reader might have missed cannot escape the eagle eye of the translator'. As a result, 'discernment and critical acumen are developed'.

But that is not enough for Pliny. Once a passage has been fully worked over, he recommends trying to compete with it. One should produce one's own account of the topic it deals with, and 'then compare your effort with the original and consider carefully where yours is better, where worse. If yours is sometimes better, congratulations; if it is worse throughout, shame on you.'

Warming to his theme, Pliny points out that, as soil is refreshed by different kinds of seed, so is our mind by different kinds of subject. So he further suggests that Fuscus try his hand at composing in different kinds of style – historical narrative and letter-writing are very helpful – and even writing poetry. 'The greatest men used to train or amuse themselves in this way – or rather, to combine training with amusement, for it is remarkable how the mind is both stimulated and relaxed by these trifles.' And Pliny goes on to explain that poetry give scope to express loves, hatreds, anger, pity and wit, 'all of which are involved in every detail of our public and professional activities'.

So that settles what our illiterate young people should be doing next year. But should it all be 'fun', as St Jerome advocated? Aristotle disagreed: 'it is clear that we are not to educate the young with a view to their amusement. While children are learning, they are not playing. Learning and pain are inseparable.'

They had been for a long time before Aristotle. Sumerian tablets dated *c.* 2000 BC (from modern Iraq) show that the foundations of education were writing (dictation and calligraphy), counting and accounting, with some language, reading and translation thrown in (students had to be familiar with everyday Akkadian and scholarly Sumerian). Physical punishment was freely employed. 'I must not be late or my teacher will beat me', we find, and beating is described as the punishment for talking, slumping over the desk, and standing up when the teacher was out of the room.

Greek and Roman education was no less violent, especially at primary school level. The Greek sketch-writer Herodas (*c.* 300-250 BC) describes what happened to the lazy little truant Coccalus, who was returned to school by his mother to be dealt with by the teacher Lampriscus. Coccalus is hoisted up on the back of another pupil, and Lampriscus calls for the 'hard leather strap, the bullock's tail I use to beat boys with'. The terrified Coccalus pleads with him to use the other strap instead, but to no avail.

The Hebrew *mûsar* means both 'education' and 'punishment', and the two seemed inseparable in ancient Mediterranean cultures. It is interesting, therefore, that the Latin word for school, *ludus*, means 'game', and our 'school' derives from Greek *scholê*, 'leisure'. 'Fun' after all?

Failing teachers

But the modern world is as bedevilled as much by *how* one teaches as *what* one teaches. As assorted OFSTEDs and Quality Assessment Agencies spend millions 'auditing' teaching and downgrading those who do not, for example, have the correct design of hand-outs, set compulsory dissertations, etc., one wonders what they would have made of Socrates.

Socrates set out to define 'goodness'. This would enable people to *know* what was moral and immoral. One can teach what one knows: and so one can teach people to be moral, and therefore happy. Socrates made no use of handouts, reading-lists, visual aids or eye-catching notice boards (he did occasionally draw in the sand), but relied on labour-intensive small-group discussion. Admitting to ignorance of what 'goodness' was, he spent most of the time trying to find out from students. Records, seating-plans, lectures, essays and assessment procedures played no part. His only stated aims and objectives were to leave students more baffled at the end of the lesson than they were at the start. He had no respect for authority, and abused visiting lecturers and politicians regardless of status.

His research record was abysmal. Though he made one breakthrough in discipline theory – that no one goes wrong willingly – he never found out what 'goodness' was and published nothing. Indeed, the only positive thing that could be said for him was that, since he refused to be paid and made no use of 'resources' of any sort, he was not a drain on the economy. Quality Assessors, obediently ticking boxes, would certainly have recommended him for dismissal – or redeployment into an administrative cost-cutting unit.

Or they might have thrown him into prison. For the association of aristocratic education with pederasty in the Greek world was absolute (see pp. 5, 120). Originally *gymnasia* consisted of little more than an open space, with a water supply and shrine. Plato's dialogue *Charmides* gives a good idea of what went on there. Socrates, who has just returned from military service and wants to catch up on things, turns up at the wrestling ground eager to find out 'if any young man has become pre-eminent in wisdom or beauty or both', and has the young Charmides pointed out to him. He is stunningly good-looking ('Wait till he strips', leers Chairephon, 'you won't notice his face') and young and old alike cannot take their eyes off him. But he has a persistent headache, and Socrates begs an introduction on the grounds that he knows a good headache cure. Charmides is beckoned over and everyone pushes and shoves along the bench to get the young man to sit by them, but eventually he settles down beside Socrates who takes a glance at what is inside Charmides' cloak and admits to being set on fire by it. But being made of sterner stuff, responsive to the inner rather than the outer man, Socrates immediately rallies and begins to engage Charmides in an earnest philosophical discussion on the nature of *sôphrosunê*, 'self-control', and they chunter on happily about this for the rest of the dialogue, reaching (as usual) no conclusion. No more is said about the headache.

To us, this is bewildering, if not disgusting, knowing as we do the grim effects of child-abuse on the young. To the Greeks it was as natural as breathing. These days, of course, we have philosophical *cafés* (the rage started in France) which are less threatening to the young. Even so, there is a strong case for exercising mind and body rather than mind and digestive system. Perhaps we need philosophical health clubs, where alongside all those horrible running-machines and weights you can develop a washboard dialectic, tone up slack cognitive theories and then relax in the *mens sana*.

MORAL DEBATE

A major problem facing educationists today is whether morality itself can be taught. But this raises much larger issues. Ancient Greeks took it for granted that discussion of values could take place only within the context of rational discussion about what society was for. The point is that for Greeks, goodness, *aretê*, carried with it strong overtones of moral *and political* wisdom (see p. 77).

Socrates raises the whole question of teaching moral standards in Plato's dialogue *Protagoras*. Here Socrates points out that in the citizen Assembly, only properly trained experts speak on technical matters; but on matters of e.g. policy, requiring value judgements, anyone can speak, when clearly they have never been taught 'policy' or 'values' in their lives. Likewise, Athens' best citizens often pay for expensive educations for their sons, who then turn out corrupt: evidently neither schools nor parents can teach them those elusive moral standards.

Protagoras replies that *aretê* – which he defines as respect for others and a sense of justice – has been acquired because it is essential to human survival. Without learning to take concerted action, humans could never have learned to live in communities and defend themselves against hostile external forces. So all men possess *aretê* by simple virtue of being human, or the state would not exist. Indeed, in the unlikely event that anyone entirely lacking it were to be found, he would have to be put to death. But since everyone possesses it to different degrees, everyone is also capable of improvement.

To prove that Athenians think *aretê* can be taught, Protagoras goes on, consider how they continually correct and punish wrongdoers, clearly because they think this will remedy defects and teach goodness. Further, good men *do* try to educate their sons in it. Sons receive moral instruction at home and at school. The state provides laws as patterns of behaviour, and the community by its own example (since it exists as a community only by individuals' possession of *aretê*) cannot but impart it.

Why then do the sons of good men so often turn out bad? Pretend, says Protagoras, that the existence of the state depended on everyone playing the *aulos* (oboe). Everyone would be taught to achieve some competence, but you would not thereby automatically expect the son of a superb *aulos*-player to turn out like his father. It would depend on his talent. So even the most wicked son would not be absolutely so: indeed, he would look a positive Goody Two Shoes compared with anyone who really did lack *aretê*. So everyone, Protagoras concludes, has some *aretê*, and can be taught more. But to demand to know who actually teaches it is like asking who taught you your native language.

For the Greek philosopher Aristotle, meanwhile, man was a political animal – one who lived in a *polis* (city-state). So when Aristotle thought about e.g. education, he first decided what the state's duty to its citizens was (to help them lead self-sufficient and *aretê*-driven existences) and then what form of state could best deliver this ideal (one ruled by an enlightened monarch; failing that, aristocrats of *aretê*; failing them, some limited form of democracy).

The contrast with western thought is telling. Today's prevailing ethos is that the world is populated by autonomous individuals, beholden to no one, doing their own thing as of right, without reference to any other norms than their own feelings and desires. If the purpose of society is to allow this ethos to flourish, there will be little point in the government attempting to impose moral education upon it (cf. p. 15).

Arty-Hearties: Arts, Drama and Games

TECHNICAL ARTS

Any discussion of the arts tends to contrast modern 'creativity' with historical 'traditionalism'. Such conflicts meant little to ancient Greeks. There was no clash between tradition and modernism. Greek artists worked within well-defined limits, producing work for private and public admiration on a restricted number of topics (in sculpture, for example, gods and heroes). The tension in their work arises from reconciling pattern and proportion with ever more accurate representation. Creativity was of no importance.

This does not mean Greek art stood still. Far from it. But experimentation took place strictly within the context of existing conventions. So Greeks absorbed eastern subject-matter and techniques, but slowly. Artists themselves were seen primarily as technicians (Plutarch calls them 'servile'), to be judged not on their 'sincerity' or 'gender-awareness', let alone their 'ability to express themselves' (why should anyone be interested in the thoughts of a technician, except on technical matters?), but, like a dentist or car-mechanic, on results, and the public expected high technical standards coupled with successful answers to new technical problems. There was no trembling reverence for the 'artist', or interest in his views on, for example, social deprivation. As Plutarch points out, 'No one of good breeding or high ideals feels they must be an artist after seeing the work of (the Athenian sculptor) Pheidias, or a poet because they get so much pleasure out of poetry. It does not follow that, because a particular work succeeds in charming us, its creator also demands our admiration.' So there would have been no TV chat-shows with artists unfolding their fascinating views about the world of ancient Greece.

The artist, in other words, was a servant of the public. That is why the common man was so appreciative of the arts, and artists were so careful about innovation and experiment. Art was not for art's sake, but the consumers'. In the fiercely competitive world of ancient Greece, no patron was going to risk his reputation on someone who would invite ridicule.

Packaging the past

So there were specific ways of doing things in the ancient world,
encouraging artists to draw on rich traditions. The Roman Vitruvius
(first century BC), for example, produced a 10-book *de architectura*,
based firmly on the Greek tradition, to show young architects how to
proceed. This book of best practice was to provide principles for centuries to come. Vitruvius deals with urban styles (terraces, stoas,
peristyles); public monuments (forum, temple, theatre, baths); and
domestic architecture from the grand villa to the farmyard (oxen in
stalls facing the sunrise, please). This standardised packaging of features that produces such yelps of horror from modern architects was
Vitruvius' way of ensuring that the best of the past was handed on to
the future, with 'success guaranteed' stamped on it.

One especially interesting feature of ancient architecture is the
Caryatid. These were female citizens of Greek Caryae, who (it is said)
were sold into slavery when their city (which defected to the Persians
during the Persian wars of 490-479 BC) was punished and destroyed. To
remind the world of this defection, architects turned the Caryatids into
load-bearing features of their buildings so that they would be forever
seen burdened with the weight of their shame. One is tempted by the
thought that all modern buildings should have a compulsory similar
feature, with the architects responsible taking the Caryatids' place.

Curse of the purse

In Great Britain, the arts go hand in hand with 'underfunding'. That is
because the arts have become an offshoot of the welfare state, so that
everyone has a 'right' to them, and the country has a 'duty' to support
artists in the same way as hospitals (and also to impose new govern-
ment-controlled quality assessment procedures on them, which will, of
course, be a tremendous help). None of this applied in the ancient
world, where art was commissioned by private patrons or publicly
funded as part of a state's religious obligations. Greeks certainly adored
the visual and performing arts. Temples and monuments were richly
decorated with paintings and sculpture. Dance, music and poetry were
at the heart of their religious festivals, and system of education (see
p. 126). Even so they sometimes balked at the expense. When the
Athenian people refused to vote funds to complete the Parthenon
(finally finished 432 BC), their leader Pericles threatened to privatise the
project, complete it himself, and call it the Pericleion.

Not that this meant that ancient buildings were put up any more efficiently than ours are. Hadrian's Wall was started in AD 122 as a simple holding line. It was redesigned to a narrower gauge in AD 124. Someone then decided to add garrisons. Someone else thought a ditch would be a good idea. Twenty years later it was abandoned. Regarrisoning and abandonment went on till *c.* AD 400.

The world record for delayed buildings is probably held by the gigantic temple of Olympian Zeus in Athens. It was started in the Doric style by the sixth-century BC Athenian tyrant Peisistratus (to keep the people too busy to indulge in plots, Aristotle claims), but abandoned soon after, with only part of the base laid. In 174 BC work resumed, this time in the Corinthian order, but only the shafts and capitals were erected, and in 86 BC a number of these were taken back to Rome by the Roman general Sulla. It was finally finished by the Roman emperor Hadrian *c.* AD 130, complete with a gold and ivory statue of Zeus (copied from Pheidias' fifth-century BC original in Olympia) and a modestly colossal one of himself, nearly seven hundred years after its original commissioning.

Luvvies' lament

For Plato, however, the arts could not be under-funded enough. Since he believed life itself was merely a pale shadow of something much higher, artists were simply creating the shadow of a shadow – doubly removed from reality. As Plato said, if artists could choose to make both the copy and the real thing, who would choose to make the copy? The arts therefore pretended to a status they did not possess.

Second, the arts were immoral. Well before Plato, there had been a lengthy debate about poets' tendency to lie. The philosopher Xenophanes (*c.* 570-470 BC), for example, complained that Homer attributed to the gods everything that men find blameworthy – theft, adultery and deceit. Plato agreed, and added that the arts also excited all that was worst in people. Tragedies, mere *acting*, made the audience burst into tears and lament; at comedies, they applauded what was silly and vulgar. The arts, then, perverted rather than enhanced people's emotions.

Plato had no time for theories about 'art for art's sake', or the arts having their own rules and values independent of everyday life, or that there was more to art than representation. Merely giving pleasure was not enough. Without close moral supervision, the arts were indefensible. Aristotle, who enjoyed running battles with Plato on most things, took a different view, arguing that the purpose of art was to encapsulate life, indeed, to represent it at a more intense, concentrated level than life itself ever could. But one can rather see Plato's point, given the extraordinary emotional effect the arts can have, particularly music.

Greeks were especially aware of the power of music to change the disposition of those who heard it. Acolytes of the Greek mystic philosopher Pythagoras (sixth century BC) claimed to have developed a form of music therapy. When they got up in the morning, songs and pieces for the lyre prepared them for the rigours of the day, and when they went to bed, purged them of all cares and prepared them for prophetic dreams. Some believed that certain types of music could cure illness like fainting, epilepsy, sciatica and snake-bites. There were incantations to induce and help on labour. An unknown painter said that he achieved the best likenesses when someone was singing to the lyre.

There was also some agreement on the moral influence of music on the listener. The 'Dorian mode' was held to be the most dignified and solemn. Plato thought it mirrored the character of the man who was brave in battle, self-controlled and hardy. This, naturally, was the first mode young Greeks learnt at school. The 'Phrygian mode' (on the pipe) accompanied religious frenzy and orgies. The 'Lydian mode' was slack and soft, ideal for the symposium (drinking party). When Pythagoras came across a young man flown with drink, love, jealousy and Phrygian pipe music, and about to set fire to his mistress's door, he saved the situation by ordering the piper to play a more dignified melody.

Copycats

In strong contrast with the modern world's passion for 'creativity' and artists' jealous protection of their own artistic output, it comes as no surprise to observe that ancient artists were plagiarists, or rather 'creative imitators', to a man. They wanted to learn from the best that was available. Homer, for example, composer of the *Iliad* and *Odyssey* (the West's first literature), set the standards for epic, and some 700 years later, Virgil wrote his *Aeneid* (29-19 BC) so as to invite comparison – so much so, in fact, that some people complained of him 'pilfering Homer'. His hero Aeneas leaves burning Troy and sets out on the high seas for many an adventure with woman and monster, including a trip to the Underworld, before reaching Italy (Homer's Odysseus did exactly the same in order to return home to Ithaca when the Trojan war was over); then Aeneas, arrived in Italy, has to fight to establish his authority over the locals, and succeeds only after much loss of life, including that of the boy entrusted to his care, Pallas (compare the fighting around Troy in the *Iliad* and the Greek hero Achilles' loss of his beloved Patroclus).

From the sublime to the ridiculous: Roman comedy also took its cue entirely from Greek comedy. This was not the rumbunctious Athenian Aristophanes. His so-called 'Old Comedy' with its contemporary, lunatic plots, rich obscenities and slashing, often vicious attacks on politicians, intellectuals, officials and anyone else he could get a laugh out of, especially other dramatists, died with the passing of Athenian independence and democracy during the fourth century BC. It was Menander (*c*. 342-292 BC) and his contemporaries, exponents of apolitical comedies of manners and 'romantic' love, involving sighing lovers, angry old fathers, swapped babies and tricky slaves who caught the attention of Roman comedians like Plautus (*c*. 250-184 BC).

Naturally, Plautus does not just translate Greek into Latin. Like Virgil, he takes his material and moulds it to his purpose. This is especially true of his tricky slaves. Talkative, boastful, inventive, witty, impudent, scurrilous they are larger-than-life figures, looking forward to P.G. Wodehouse's Jeeves, the Steptoes and Baldrick. They revel in tricking the cash out of the curmudgeonly father or nasty pimp to get the girl for their young master. There is nothing like them in Menander.

In Plautus' *Bacchides*, for example, the slave Chrysalus, having once already been caught out trying to filch the money by the suspicious old father, sets up a second deception with a brilliant bogus letter begging for the cash. It is superb moment when he pleads with the father not to be fooled by this letter, let alone to give him (Chrysalus) the money to transport to his feckless son. ('No, if you're wise you won't pay up. And *I* won't take it. No, I'm tired of your slurs on my honesty. Find someone else. No, don't trust me with it ... No! Oh all right, if you *must* ...').

The Roman lyric poet Horace (65-8 BC) worked in just the same way with Greek lyric poetry, the Roman love poet Catullus (*c*. 84-54 BC) with Greek love poetry. Potters, sculptors and architects took years learning to imitate the work of their predecessors before taking on commissions of their own. They had to learn what worked: only previously successful pieces could tell them.

Ancient artists naturally loved it if someone obviously cribbed them. It showed how superior they were. Aristophanes was always boasting to his audiences how other comedians had whipped his best lines and plots; Martial made amusing epigrams out of his refusal to send his latest collection of poems to rival poets because he claimed they would recite them as if they were their own. He makes modern literary invective sound like the speaking clock. Poets recited their work before publishing it ('Why do you put a scarf round your neck when you recite? It would be better round our ears') and accusations of envy and plagiarism were rife: 'Paulus buys poetry, and recites it as his. Well, he did buy it: *surely* he can call it his own?' Then there was Cinna: 'Cinna is said to be writing verses against me. But how can you tell he's writing? Nobody reads him.' Varus was a congenital non-performer: 'You write two hundred lines a day, but never recite a thing. Idiot! Or perhaps not ....' Martial thanked another poet for returning his latest book unopened: 'Yes, of *course* you read it. I believe you. I know. I'm glad. It's true. That's the way I've read *your* last five books.'

Philistine note

Amid all this ancient passion for the arts, echoed by Prime Minister Blair's 'Cool Britannia', grovelling in slack-jawed adulation before the stupendously important achievements of a job lot of fashion designers, hair-stylists and film directors, the ancient Greek man of letters Plutarch offers a dissenting voice.

In his essay 'Why were the Athenians famous?', Plutarch looks back on the astonishing achievements that made fifth-century Athens 'the mother and kindly nurse of the arts, some of which she was the first to discover and realise, while others she developed and advanced'. Great artists and historians vied with each other 'to make a vivid representation of emotions and characters', the one in paints, the other with words, e.g. the historian Thucydides, who wrote 'to make the reader a spectator' and to produce in his mind the same feelings that were experienced by those who actually witnessed the events.

Then there were the poets. Plutarch talks warmly of the 'blossoming forth' of tragedy and the 'great acclaim it won, becoming a wonderful entertainment for the ears and eyes of that age by the mythological character of its plots and the vicissitudes of fortune of its characters'. He mentions 'the wisdom of Euripides, the eloquence of Sophocles and the nobility of Aeschylus' (fifth-century BC tragic poets) and tells the famous story of the drawing-room comedian Menander who, asked whether he had finished his latest comedy yet, replied 'Yes. The plot's in order. All I have to do now is write the words.'

And what, Plutarch goes on, a total waste of time. Did historians ever do anything but record? Did tragedy bring to Athens, he argues, anything to compare with the achievements of Miltiades and Themistocles in saving the city from the Persians (in the Persian wars, 490-479 BC), and of Pericles in having the Parthenon built (447-432 BC)? Did tragedies rid Athens of any of its difficulties, or gain for her any brilliant successes? How can one compare the records of victories at the dramatic festivals with memorials of valour and heroism? Let tragedians, he says, bring on their stage equipment, their masks and altars, their actors, choruses and beautiful robes – all emptiness and vanity, 'an oblation to their wasted livelihood'.

And that about classical Athens! What would Plutarch have made of the drivelling mobs of crooners and restaurant decorators that Mr Blair so recently worshipped as modern Britain's crowning glory?

FAMILY TRAGEDIES

Any catastrophe today involving the deaths of the innocent is usually called a 'tragedy'. But tragedies do not occur naturally. They are literary products.

The Roman poet Horace ascribed the invention of tragedy to the Athenian Thespis (sixth century BC). Whatever *trag-ôidia* meant (literally 'a song to do with a goat', *tragos*), by the end of the fifth century BC Aeschylus, Sophocles and Euripides had explored the genre so conclusively that it needed a Shakespeare to take it further.

Greek tragedy is astonishingly various. There is Oedipus in Sophocles, blinding himself after discovering that, for all his efforts, he has fulfilled the oracles by killing his father and marrying his mother; and there is the almost comic Euripides' *Helen*, when, after the Trojan war, Helen's husband Menelaus stumbles weed-covered ashore in Egypt to find Helen was there all along and the Trojan war had been fought over a wraith.

But for all its variety, tragedians regularly chose the darkest of these ancient myths to try to explore extremes of human behaviour. In awesome figures like Oedipus, Clytaemnestra and Medea, the tragedians searched for meaning, or at least patterns, intelligible to fifth-century Greeks. But whose tragedy was it? Both victim's and perpetrator's: often gods or oracles ensured that they were fatally, and ironically, enmeshed from an early stage, and found out too late.

So Greek tragedians could have made little out of, for example, the Dunblane massacre. There were no heroes, oracles, gods, dramatic reversals or ironic revelations, let alone interaction of agent and victims. Tragedians often looked to the Furies or heaven-sent madness to 'explain' events. But even these usually worked to some inscrutable purpose. There was, sadly, no purpose, however inscrutable, in Dunblane.

It was to the family that Greek tragedians usually looked for their subject-matter. Greeks were all too aware of the terrifying forces latent there – as we are. A large percentage of murders today involve family members, often a father or even mother killing their young children because of a divorce and separation. The destructiveness of the family, murder and incest in particular, was a major topic of Greek myth.

Oedipus, for example, killed his father and married his mother. Medea, abandoned by her husband Jason, killed their two children and his new bride as well. Thyestes seduced his brother Atreus' wife; Atreus took his revenge by serving up Thyestes' sons to him in a casserole at dinner. Atreus' son Agamemnon sacrificed his own daughter Iphigeneia to gain the wind that would take the Greek fleet to Troy. When he returned triumphant from Troy, his wife Clytaemnestra cut him down in the bath, only for herself to be killed later in turn by their son Orestes.

The point is that no institution was of more importance to Greeks than the family: everything they held dear centred on it (see pp. 6-7). Since nothing therefore had greater potential for tragic consequences, Greek tragedians fastened on myths of the family and explored what it took for a man or woman to hate what was most precious to them with such a passion as to destroy it. Sometimes, for example, they shaped an explanation around the desire for revenge (Medea); ignorance (Oedipus); a family curse (Agamemnon); an error of judgement (Aristotle's *hamartia*); or an abstract force like 'delusion' or 'madness'. Nor could the will of the gods be discounted as an element in the equation. But humans were never cleared of responsibility for what they had done.

So when bright young modern playwrights put sexual perversions and baby-eating on the stage because they 'want to tell the truth about human behaviour', one feels like pointing out that this 'truth' has been around for some time. Further, one feels like asking whether mere 'events' are necessarily 'drama'. Aristotle famously identifies six crucial elements necessary to a drama: plot-structure, character, reasoning (by which he seems to mean arguments and emotions), verbalisation, song (all ancient drama had a musical element) and visual design. He would ask, for example, whether the plot was 'necessary' or 'probable'. Are the characters 'lifelike' and 'consistent'? Does the dramatist use spectacle merely 'to produce what is only monstrous'? As Aristotle insists, the best dramatist could cut the spectacle and still produce the same effects. Further, he assigned the origins of all literary composition to humans' love of imitation. It is, he argues, how children learn their first lessons. Bright young playwrights are obviously at this elementary stage, imitating the subjects of Greek myth. Aristotle could help them become dramatists.

The flavour of lowerbrow

But a word of warning is in order. When we think of classical drama, we tend to think of solemn Greek tragedy or Aristophanes' comedies. These were, indeed, highly popular, and taken round the Greek world for performance in competitions at local theatres after their showing at the great Lenaia and Dionysia festivals in Athens (that is why there are theatres all over the Greek world). One should not, however, forget another staple dramatic fare of Greeks and Romans: mime and pantomime (this latter used no words), played by local or travelling companies, often in competitions, and strongly resembling the sort of thing we enjoy during the Christmas period. Though little survives, we can say with confidence that it would have given modern TV a pretty tough run for its money.

Mime took many forms – song-and-dance routines, parodies of everyday life (e.g. the ruined party, the escaping adulterer, the rejected lover, the wife who tries to poison her husband to have it off with her slaves) and schmaltzy melodrama bursting with human interest (we hear of a mime set in India, where the lovely heroine escapes with the help of her brother by making the king and his court drunk). There was no restriction on the number or sex of the actors (as there was in tragedy and comedy). Explicit sexual themes were very prominent. Famous mime artists were wildly popular and made a fortune, and Roman emperors like Augustus (a great fan) staged mime frequently to keep the people happy (but cracked down on artists who tried to use it for political purposes). Even non-dramatic texts could be converted to mime – we hear of mimes of the Roman poet Virgil's pastoral ramblings, the *Eclogues* (38 BC).

It is tempting to think that Mr and Mrs Average Greek's idea of a good day at the theatre was Aeschylus' *Oresteia* followed by an intensive discussion of Aeschylus' concept of fate or the use of the mask. *Women Behaving Badly* is an equally likely option.

Artistic conflict

The endlessly dreary Oscar/BAFTA/Emmy ceremonies attract phe-
nomenal interest, when all they usually consist of is various dim artistes
awarding prizes to other even dimmer artistes and the whole world
convulsed with excitement. But ancient Greeks would certainly have
been up there convulsing with them.

Greeks adored competitions, which were put on at festival times to
celebrate some religious occasion. Games were hugely popular. The
Olympics were the big one, forming what was known as 'the circuit'
with the Nemean, Isthmian and Pythian (Delphic) Games, but these
were only four out of hundreds of similar occasions celebrated all over
the Greek world. Choral song-and-dance competitions were equally
popular and fiercely contested. Tragedies and comedies were staged
only in competition against each other. The two big drama festivals in
Athens in honour of Dionysus, god of drama, were the Lenaia
(January) and Dionysia (April), and dramatists competed fiercely to
have their plays selected for them (shown just the once, and then going
on tour to local festival competitions). 'Best Producer' and 'Best Actor'
prizes were also awarded, the latter on the strength of audience accla-
mation.

In the hot-house of competition at the theatre, the crowd tried to
influence the judges by indicating how it felt about the performances,
often while they were still going on. Indeed, the audience could
become so violent that attendants with whips patrolled the theatre. The
most common form of abuse was hissing and hooting, accompanied by
heels kicking against the seats. Plato complained that it had got so bad
that the crowd had established a sort of boxofficeocracy over the
theatre. Plutarch tells us that by his time (second century AD) actors
needed claques to support them in case the crowd did not like their
interpretation.

Everyone concerned with the production – actors, singers, author,
sponsor – was a target for audience abuse. They could be hissed off in
mid-performance (we hear of an occasion when one comedy after
another was brought to a halt as a result of this treatment) or forcibly
thrown out of the theatre. In his *Characters*, Theophrastus (fourth-
third century BC) describes the 'Yobbo' as one who hissed while others
applauded and applauded while others remained silent (unless he
decided to emit a loud belch instead), and the 'Cretin' as one who slept
soundly during the performance and remained asleep long after the
theatre had emptied.

Multi-media

But even in Greek times top luvvies commanded a tremendous following. By the fourth century BC some Greek actors were so famous that they were employed as diplomats and by the third century BC actors had formed themselves into guilds, modestly calling themselves 'Artists of Dionysus' (some called them 'Parasites'). They negotiated freedom of travel and immunity from military service, and competed at festivals everywhere. Inscriptions for a big festival competition at Delphi list 251 artists, including 40 from Corinth, 29 from Athens, 57 from Boeotia, 11 from Asia Minor and 10 from the Black Sea.

True to the great trade union tradition of solidarity, different guilds clashed constantly with each other. Corinthian artists, for example, claimed the right to exclude Athenians from some competitions. This finally ended in the first century AD, when a world-wide guild was formed, imposing strict terms and conditions of performance for their members. By the third century AD, this guild had joined forces with the Guild of Athletes – rather like Frank Bruno performing in a panto – and won exemption from taxation. This move brought bogus members flooding in, until the emperor Diocletian (284-305 AD) decreed that exemption be granted only to members who had won three crowns in major competitions. But socially, actors were still regarded as a slightly dodgy lot. One authority asks why they were so depraved, and replies 'because they have to work for a living and lack self-discipline' (see p. 2).

The combination of the actors' guild with the athletes' made good sense because Greeks thoroughly approved of combining culture with games. Both were part of the worship of the gods, who appreciated competition (see p. 163) and all forms of human excellence. So at sporting gatherings in the ancient world (as at many religious festivals), people were also entertained with a wide range of artistic performances – poetry (which combined song and dance), plays, lectures, discussions and so on. It was all a part of the popular civic and religious routine.

We are coming round to this idea. Before big sporting events these days, there is every chance that a bit of culture will be throw in with various large tenors belting out numbers from operas and selections of pop songs. As early as the fourth century BC we hear of selections from some of tragedies' greatest arias being performed solo, and the Roman emperor Nero was an avid fan.

Nero – hero or zero?

The Greek word for 'contest' is *agôn*, whence our 'agony', and intense competitiveness informed all areas of Greek life, not just the theatre (competition was divinely approved – see p. 163). Law-courts, politics, and intellectual life were just a few of the other areas where Greeks strove to come out top (see pp. 52, 43). Herodotus tells the story of the Greek attempt to select 'Best Commander' after they had defeated the Persians in the famous sea battle off Salamis in 480 BC. The commanders all met together and put the issue to the vote at the altar of the sea god Poseidon at the Isthmus. Naturally they all voted for themselves, but the Greeks had invented the single transferable vote, and it emerged that each commander had also put Themistocles second. That, sensibly, made no odds (Greeks did not give people prizes for coming *second*), and the meeting split up with no decision made. Themistocles then went to Sparta to see if he could be honoured there. While the local boy Eurybiades inevitably won 'Best Commander', the Spartans hastily invented a new category, 'Wisest Commander' (with the same olive wreath prize), and Themistocles duly won that. When it came to prizes, Greeks never gave up.

Neither did the infamous Nero. He was crazy about the arts. Early on he took up the lyre so that he could accompany himself on it, and kept his voice in trim by diet and slimming and his weight down with enemas and emetics. He made his singing debut in Naples, where he disregarded an earthquake to complete his performance (the theatre collapsed soon afterwards). He did not fiddle while Rome burnt, but, as the historian Suetonius tells us, sang. Enraptured by the beauty of the flames, he put on his tragedian's clothes (Suetonius wrote) and worked his way through 'The Fall of Troy' from beginning to end.

He put his name down for all the musical contests, in one instance singing the complete opera *Niobe* without a break so that no one else had time to compete. He promptly held the award-ceremony over for a year so that he could perform again next time. He sponsored an immense variety of entertainments, persuading the Great and Good to take part (one rode an elephant down a sloping tight-rope, others fought in the arena). He staged a naval battle complete with sea monsters, and a ballet of Daedalus and Icarus, in which Icarus fell rather too realistically, spattering Nero with blood.

Dissatisfied, however, with entertaining dull Romans, he took himself off to Greece where the arts were really appreciated. The Greeks gave him a rapturous welcome wherever he went, sending him the prizes in advance – which convinced him the Greeks really knew about art. No one was allowed to leave theatres when he performed. Women gave birth during his recitals, we are told, and people climbed out over the rear wall or shammed dead in order to be carried out. He sang on every possible public occasion. When merely making speeches on government business, however, he had a voice-trainer on hand at all times to advise him on sparing his throat or protecting his precious vocal chords with a handkerchief. He adored chariot racing, driving a ten-horse team at Olympia but failing to finish the course. It made no difference – he still got the prize. When a coup removed him from power and he was persuaded to commit suicide, his famous last words were *qualis artifex pereo* – 'Dead! And what an artist!' Our modern ministers of culture have a lot to live up to.

Clash of the bottoms

On the other hand, perhaps our ministers are taking too close an interest in the arts, at least at Westminster. At one stage, evidently, a secret snapper was cruising the Houses of Parliament taking pictures of MPs' rears for a Beautiful Bottoms competition. Aphrodite, goddess of sex, would have thoroughly approved: one of her cult titles was *Kallipygos* – 'lovely-buttocked'.

She was given this title, the Greek essayist Athenaeus tells us, when two poor sisters, each convinced her bottom was the fairer, invited a passing youth, son of a rich man, to judge. He selected the elder sister, fell violently in love, and had to go home and lie down. He told his younger brother, however, who decided a second opinion was needed. He selected the younger and also fell in love. They all got married and the two now wealthy sisters gratefully dedicated a shrine to Aphrodite *Kallipygos*.

Bottom contests then became quite the fashion. Alciphron (c. AD 200) describes a fine example of such a competition between two courtesans, Myrrhina and Thryallis, at a drinking party. The question was – whose bottom was softer? Myrrhina, clothed in a silk see-through shift, stood up and, turning her head back to keep a firm eye on her buttocks, shook them 'till they quivered like a junket', moaning softly all the time as if she were making love. Thryallis at once threw off what clothes she had and, sticking her bottom out, invited the audience to admire its purity, its perfect shape (not too fat or thin), how elegantly integrated with rosy hips and thighs, and well dimpled. She then vibrated her buttocks so fast that they seemed to flow like water around her hips – and won the prize. Hip, breast and belly competitions then followed, but Alciphron goes into no details.

So there is fine ancient precedent for bottom competitions, and in these liberated days, there is no reason why male and female MPs should not compete together. It will give jobless back-benchers a meaning to existence, and Sir Edward Heath can storm up the popularity ratings by volunteering to judge.

POLITICAL GAMES

Ancient Greeks got at least three things right about the Olympic Games, in strong contrast to their modern imitations.

First, so many new Games are added today that one is never certain whether one is watching an actual Game or just e.g. people squabbling over a ball (two-a-side beach-ball). Ballroom-dancing and surfing were recently invited by the International Olympic Committee to undergo a two-year trial in preparation for provisional acceptance into the Games. But Greeks, on the other hand, were deeply conservative about what was permitted.

The Games began in 776 BC, and by 520 BC the basic cannon of thirteen events had been established (foot, horse and chariot races, boxing, wrestling, pankration, and pentathlon), lasting almost untouched till at least AD 261. The first Olympic Game consisted only of a 200 metre sprint. The 400 metres was added in 724 BC, the 4800 metres in 720 BC and it was 708 BC before the first non-running event was instituted: the pentathlon (discus, standing long-jump, javelin, wrestling and 200 metres). Boxing followed in 688 BC (horribly bloody, fought without a break), chariot racing in 680 BC, horse-racing and the pankration (all-in, but no biting or gouging) in 648 BC, boys' 200 metres and wrestling (632 BC), boys' boxing (616 BC), and the race in armour (520 BC).

For the next nine hundred years, however, till the Games were ended by official edict of the Christian emperor Theodosius I in AD 393, only seven new games were introduced. Four of these were merely variations on the existing horse-racing theme and one was the boys' pankration, but the two others seem rather more controversial: a competition for heralds, and a competition for trumpeters – details of both unknown. And at least one game in that period was dropped. In 500 BC a race was introduced between pairs of mules pulling seated drivers on carts, but was abandoned in 444 BC. 'Not ancient nor dignified' says our source Pausanias. What would he have said of two-a-side beach volleyball, one wonders?

Race in full armour

Second, athletes competed as individuals, not in teams as we do today. They were all professionals, often locally financed, making good prize money on the extensive Games' circuit, and they came to Olympia to try their luck at the big one. True, the victor there won nothing more than a crown of wild olives, but like today, it was the spin-offs that counted. The result of individual entry was that it was possible to win without competing at all, as many athletes, especially in contact sports, boasted on their victory monuments, saying that they had won *akoniti*, 'without dust' i.e. their opponents took one look at them and, knowing they had no chance, sloped off. Individual, not national, entries, with permission for withdrawal, would save everyone (especially smaller countries) a great deal of expense, effort and humiliation and spectators much tedium if they were allowed today.

Finally, whereas we endure endless fatuous and corrupt competitions between cities to decide where the next Games will be held (almost a Game in itself), in Greece there was never any argument. Despite grim spectator facilities, for over a thousand years, without a break, the games were held at Olympia, the shrine of Zeus Olympios (king of the Olympian gods), in Elis (north-west Peloponnese). The men of Elis were expert organisers, officials and judges and the Olympics were known as the fairest of all the *c.* 300 Games' festivals.

Such a development nowadays would depoliticise our Games. This was not an issue in the ancient world. Elis was a backwater, of no importance at all. On top of that, when the three Greek 'sacred heralds' spread out from Elis to announce the forthcoming Games (*not* carrying an Olympic flame), they proclaimed a truce for up to three months before and after the 5-day event. Its purpose was not political (war was endemic in the Greek world) but social: to ensure safe passage for the myriad Greeks from all over the Mediterranean who travelled to watch. Only open warfare by or against the people of Elis was actually forbidden during the truce (in 364 BC an invasion by Arcadia did interrupt the pentathlon). The result was that the Games were celebrated every four years for over a thousand years, an astonishing record (compare the modern Olympics, instituted 1896 and already cancelled three times by war – 1916, 1940 and 1944). So to depoliticise the modern Games, scrap the International Committee and organise the Games locally, in the same backwater year after year, preferably untelevised. One may object: backwaters don't have the infrastructure. Neither did Olympia. How about Benbecula?

This sporting life

In fact the thuggish horribleness of the modern Olympics (and now even the World Chess Championships) makes one yearn for an outbreak of those exquisite ironies that so enlivened ancient games. For example, Milo, a Greek wrestler from Croton in South Italy (sixth century BC), was (after Heracles) the most famous strong man in the ancient world. He would bind cords round his forehead and holding his breath 'till the veins in his forehead swelled with blood' burst them. He once carried a four-year old bull round the stadium at Olympia, killed it and ate it in a day. He met his end when he tried to hold apart a tree-trunk which had been split open and was fixed with wedges. The wedges fell away, Milo's fingers were caught inside, and thus trapped he was consumed by wild animals. Polydamas, an all-in wrestler (fifth century BC), killed lions with his bare hands and once attacked a bull, which escaped only when it tore off the hoof by which Polydamas was holding on to it. He died when he proudly tried to hold up a collapsing mountain cave in which he and friends had taken shelter from the summer heat.

Greeks, with their untameable desire to win, saw games as an analogy of life. Pindar, for example, the fifth-century court poet who celebrated his patrons' victories at the games, characterised winning at Olympia as the closest one could get to divine bliss, but warned that life could not continue like that. He pointed the moral with myths of great heroes who scaled the heights only to fall (see p. 105). They were right: how one prays for modern 'sporting' thugs to be equally struck down.

All or nothing

On the other hand, when Cable TV threatens to bring American monstrosities like 'Ultimate Fighting' to the screen – a form of all-in wrestling in which only eye-gouging and biting are forbidden – who needs irony? It is only ancient Greek fighting re-heated. The pankration ('the all-mighty-one') was introduced into the Olympic games in 648 BC. Pankratiasts could punch, slap, elbow, kick, knee, head-butt and wrestle – but not gouge or bite. The aim was not to throw the opponent (as it was in the almost equally violent Greek wrestling) but to force submission. Since being thrown was irrelevant, much of the fighting took place on the ground. One unbeaten pankratiast was renowned for allowing his opponent to fall on top of him first of all, and getting to work from there. Since the main aim seems to have been to get a life- or limb-threatening hold on the opponent such as to induce surrender (e.g. a stranglehold, or one that threatened to break or dislocate limbs), punching was probably used only defensively (hand protection, of course, was not worn). Sostratus from Sicyon illustrates the point. He acquired the nick-name 'Mr Fingers' by aiming mainly to break those of his opponent.

The most famous pankratiast was Arrachion. Previously undefeated at Olympia, in 564 BC he found himself in a lethal neck and leg lock. Losing consciousness fast, Arrachion managed to loosen the leg-hold, kick out and dislocate his opponent's ankle. In agony, his opponent surrendered – too late. Arrachion was dead. But he *was* awarded the prize. Nasty – but not, in ancient eyes, as dangerous as boxing. Like modern doctors, Greeks understood the deadly effects of repeated blows to the head from heavy, leather-encased fists. Besides, most pankratiasts submitted before getting badly hurt. So 'Ultimate Fighting' is really rather tamely penultimate.

Gladiators

Romans (who muscled into taking part in the Greek games as they became masters of the Mediterranean from the second century BC onwards) remained impervious to such concerns as safety when it came to the very non-Olympic games they regularly enjoyed. Gladiators were mostly criminals or prisoners of war. Deserving nothing better, they were sent into the ring to provide the populace with 'fun' by killing and being killed. The emperors saw this as good government – punishing the wicked and pleasing the people all at one go – and were proud of the huge stadia they built to accommodate these spectacles (e.g. the Colosseum). Augustus, the first Roman emperor, listing the great things he did for Rome, boasts of the number of shows he put on and the number of men fighting (10,000) and animals killed (3,500) at them.

Gladiators were effectively professionals, however unwilling. They were housed in cramped cells in secure barracks, made to swear an oath to 'be burned by fire, bound in chains, beaten and die by the sword' and then put through the most rigorous training procedures, under the careful scrutiny of doctors and masseurs. Diet and muscle-building were very important. The great ancient doctor Galen (AD 129-199) saw service in the barracks, claiming to have reduced mortality considerably.

The point is that being a gladiator was rather like being a soccer player. Successful 'schools' could earn fortunes for their owners and for victorious gladiators too. For most of them it was their one chance to succeed in life. Champions had a large following, were idolised by women (Celadus was 'the girls' hero and heart-throb'), and, most important of all, could earn enough money to buy their freedom. A number of gladiatorial schools had accountants on the staff. It was big business. So when the guards at the high security Corcoran Jail in California recently amused themselves by matching prisoners against each other and making them fight while they laid bets on the outcome and egged them on, they could have been onto something of consider-able sociological interest. They should have thrown the prisons open to the crowds on these 'Gladiator Days', as they called them, put the receipts into prison improvements or pay-rises, and offered early release as prizes to the winners together with a contract to earn a living as a fighter attached to some well-known promoter. If violence is your trade, better conduct it legally.

Foul play

The Roman people enjoyed all this no less than those American guards did. So deeply ingrained was the sadistic spectacle in Roman culture that even humane writers like Cicero and Pliny the younger talked feebly of the good virile example it provided. Seneca is the first to protest against the whole institution, but not on the obvious humani-tarian grounds open to him. He argues against it in the terms familiar to us – the brutalisation of the *spectator*. In the morning they throw men to the animals, he says, but in the afternoon 'they throw them to the spectators'. Seneca grants that the gladiators deserve death, but goes on 'what crime have you committed that you should deserve to sit and watch?' He concludes, after watching such a spectacle, 'I come home more greedy, ambitious, voluptuous, cruel and inhuman.'

Purely humanitarian arguments against the contests were rare. Fighters deserved what they inflicted on each other. So with us today. Where boxers fight of their own free will, under controlled conditions, they obviously get what is coming to them. Whether their free collab-oration in the spectators' desire for violence makes the spectacle more or less degrading is a good question.

What is not in doubt is that, as cheating and foul play become rou-tine on e.g. the football pitch, today's crowds, brutalised by the behaviour of their 'heroes', respond in kind (as do the players, some of whom even attack the crowd back). Gladiatorial games could also cause crowd riots. In AD 59, the historian Tacitus reports, a gladiatorial show in Pompeii saw 'an exchange of taunts [between Pompeians and the people of nearby Nuceria, modern Nocera], characteristic of these disorderly country towns', which led to 'abuse, stone-throwing and drawn swords'. The Nucerians came off worse, and many were wounded, many killed. Graffiti and a wall-painting of the incident survive. The Roman response was to ban such shows from Pompeii for ten years and exile the sponsor. There might be a message here for our government.

Water sports

Not that Romans were unimaginative when it came to entertainment. We enjoy fantasies at Christmas – unlikely people (like Aladdin) having unlikely adventures (with genies) on unlikely terrain (ice) – and so did the Romans. Lacking refrigeration facilities, they opted for the next best thing – shows in water. Many ancient theatres have been adapted to cater for them (and for wild beast shows). The grandest of all was surely the emperor Titus' three-day inauguration of his brand new amphitheatre the Colosseum in AD 80, built on the site of Nero's artificial lake (see p. 119).

The most dramatic performances were the re-enactments of two famous Greek naval battles – Corfu *vs.* Corinth (434 BC) on the first day, and Athens *vs.* Syracuse (413 BC) on the third. Criminals manned the ships (real marines were far too precious): the more killed, the better. Then the story of Hero and Leander was performed, with Leander swimming across the water to his beloved on an island in the middle. This was staged by torch-light at night, as too was another show, synchronised swimming by naked Nereids (mythological sea-goddesses).

There followed a display of aquatic dressage in which animals including bulls and horses performed in water what they had been trained to do on land. After that came a hunt, with perhaps as many as five thousand animals being driven into the water to be dispatched, and after that a chariot race, with spray being kicked up like dust, as the poet Martial describes it. Historical sea-battles, ancient myths, aquatic chariot-races, and all in the very centre of Rome – *fantastic* (you can hear the mob preening itself). What an emperor. Real class. That's what comes of being the most powerful nation on earth.

Horse-power

The horse was the big status symbol in the ancient world, especially with a coach or chariot attached. But no Roman who owned one would ever deign to *drive* it. That was servants' work. The whole point was to be on display in it, like the emperor Claudius whose coach was fitted with a gaming room. As for racing charioteers, they might become popular heroes but they were very low in social esteem. Racing was as dangerous as today's Grand Prix. Reins wrapped round their body, with a knife to free themselves if they fell, the charioteers jockeyed for the inside position as they turned the *metae* at the ends of the circuit, and often victory was won only on the seventh lap (*septimo spatio*). There were horrifying crashes. The people supported their favourite 'colours' (Blues and Greens were popular in Rome) and Pliny tells the story of an owner who would let his home town know who had won by means of a carrier-swallow, legs painted with the victorious colour.

Roman moralists were shocked at owners who yearned in secret to drive the things themselves. Aristocrats, Romans felt, should behave like nobs, not yobs (see p. 105). The satirist Juvenal laughed at one Lateranus, who as consul confined his driving to night-time when no one but the moon could see him – he even fed and mucked out the horses himself – but when his term of office was over, went shamelessly public with his passions. Nero was crazy about horses from childhood. Even as emperor he played constantly with model ivory chariots.

So when today's youths steal cars and race them about ('hotting', as it was once called), they are getting it all wrong. Far classier to steal cars with chauffeurs, and lounge in the back while the chauffeurs do the hotting. What, after all, does *chauffeur* mean?

7

The Powers Above

BY RITES

Goddesses on Olympus such as Athene (patroness of Athens) and Artemis must find church debates about women priests quite baffling.

Ancient religious belief was designed to take into account as much of the observable world as it could. If there are trees, rocks and rivers, there must be gods of the same. Humans are male and female. There must therefore be male and female gods. Given, then, that one's aim was to keep gods happy, but one had no idea what it was that kept them happy, one hedged one's bets, and it was an obvious bet to assume that some gods would prefer to be served by females. It made sense, then, that there should be priestesses as well as priests. In Athens, virtually anyone could become a priest(ess), usually by election, sometimes by inheritance, but the idea of 'vocation' did not come into it. A priest(ess)'s function was to ensure that the ritual specific to the god whose sanctuary he or she served was properly carried out. Since the post was honorary and part-time, virginity and celibacy were not often required (far too impractical).

The temple was a place for the god to live in and rarely featured in the ritual, which took place outside, around the altar. This was the action centre of ancient religion. There was no Church, no preaching, no theology (Greeks did not have a 'Bible'), no creeds, no crèches, no dogma, no sin, no ongoing caring interaction with the wider community. Gods in general did not demand belief, love, social awareness or moral probity – only acknowledgement, in accordance with traditional rituals (see p. 118). An analogy with a force like gravity might be useful. If you fail to acknowledge it on cliff-tops, you will be in trouble, however religious.

Take the recent BSE scare in the UK. In 427 BC, so the Roman historian Livy tells us, there was a terrible drought. Many cattle perished of thirst, but others were carried off 'by a *scabies*, which was contagious and spread to humans'. At first, he tells us, it infected country-dwellers and their workers, but then it spread to Rome itself.

It did not merely affect their bodies either, 'but a horde of superstitions, mostly foreign, took possession of their minds as well'. The reason for this was that quack seers, seeing the chance to make a quick buck, encouraged the more simple-minded among the people in the belief that, if they carried out certain new sacrificial rites, they could escape contagion. As a result, mad oblation disease spread among the superstitious, and shrines and streets echoed with 'outlandish and unfamiliar sacrifices to appease the gods' anger'. When the authorities got to hear of it, they decided it was time to stop this 'public disgrace'. The aediles (in charge of city works) were empowered to see to it that only Roman gods were worshipped, and in the traditional way.

The importance of ritual to Greeks, as to Romans, lay in the protection which proper acknowledgement of the gods was thought to impart: scratch the god's back and (s)he would scratch yours. Priest(esse)s merely ensured that the community or state scratched the right place at the right time in the right way. Ancient religion was not a matter of personal choice, let alone of personal belief. As the fourth-century BC professor Isocrates said, contrasting present (degenerate) Athens with its glorious past, 'Our ancestors' concern was not to weaken the religion of their fathers or introduce unwanted innovations. So the blessings of the gods were visited on them for ploughing and for harvest each in its season with unbroken regularity.'

The idea that religion was an open house, where anyone could worship the gods in any way they chose, would have struck Greeks as suicidal. The gods were far too powerful a force to be left to individual whim. So rituals, especially the great communal ones, were carefully overseen and even reviewed after the event to ensure they had been properly carried out (see p. 118). If they had not been, those responsible could be punished and the ritual might have to be repeated. Ritual could be changed, but it was only after much careful consultation of the gods through e.g. the oracle at Delphi that a community would consider changing it in any radical way. Besides, many of the rituals were, like the Authorised Version of the Bible, extremely enjoyable. Only at a sacrifice, for example, would many Greeks eat meat. But the personalisation of religion today and its fragmentation into various creeds has eroded this idea that the safety of the whole community is at stake in the worship of God. There is as much to be said for the unifying and validating force of tradition in worship as there is in art and literature. Competition is not always a good thing.

What's in a name?

Ancients would have been baffled by the decision of the Methodist church in 1992 to allow the congregation to call God 'Mother'. Identifying the divinity correctly by name and attributes is an ancient concern, reflected in pagan and Jewish literature as well as in the Lord's Prayer: 'Our Father, which art in heaven [ah, *that* one], hallowed be thy name ...'. Thus Athene, among many other titles, was known as 'protector of the city', 'mistress of handicrafts', 'leader in battle' and 'granter of victory'. Greeks would summon her by name under the title most appropriate to their needs at the time of the prayer. The naming did not alter the nature or power of the god; all it did was to ensure the right god was being summoned, bringing appropriate powers. (To that extent, knowing the god's name and titles gave power over the god.) But just in case they had missed out an important title, Greeks and Romans frequently added the catch-all 'or by whatever other name you like to be called'. Now the god really could not refuse to come to their aid.

So the ancients would have been baffled by the Methodist decision. For Methodists there is only one God. If they want to de-sex their God, they are going a very strange way about it by assigning the god two different sexes. If they want female worshippers to feel comfortable about God, ancients would smell a rat. Feeling comfortable with the god was not the purpose of ancient religion. The ancients would sympathise only if Methodists had evidence that God was angry with them, and that the change would appease him or increase the number of Methodist worshippers. The ancient solution would be to begin all prayers 'O God, of whatever gender, genders, or none'.

SIGN LANGUAGE

Humans responded to the gods in a number of ways. As well as building temples and performing rituals, they also held festivals like the Olympic Games and drama competitions (see p. 142); made sacrifices; and prayed, using a time-honoured formula in which, standing, with hands raised to the gods above or lowered to those below, the human identified the right god for the job, outlined the need, and pointed out his own benefactions to the god in the past and/or promised some for the future, in return for which the god had an obligation to help him *now*.

Humans also consulted them. The fifth-century BC Greek philosopher-physicist Heraclitus, renowned for his enigmatic utterances, said 'God does not speak nor does he keep [things] hidden, but he gives signs'. The gods did this in many ways. For example, they could send dreams, speak through oracles, influence the flight of birds and affect the shape of an animal's liver. All such religious 'signs' required a human to interpret them properly (gods were not expected to communicate clearly). This was not the job of a priest, who was concerned with correct ritual, but of a seer, and there were families of seers who specialised in this art, though *anyone* could have a shot at it. Incidentally, it is usually only in myth that one tends to find amazing oracles with obscure double meanings and terrible warnings. The everyday reality, from what we can gather from surviving inscriptions, is mostly much duller, because the great majority of questions asked at oracles concern religious practice and not the winner of the 3.30 at Gosforth Park (Greeks were not stupid).

Come election time, newspapers do something rather similar: they spend millions of pounds on polls. These pretend to be forecasting the future. But they are doing nothing of the sort. They cannot foretell the future: they merely indicate how people are thinking on that day. If they want to foretell the future, papers may as well take auspices – wingometers in place of swingometers.

Or, perhaps, not. Romans, for example, used auspices not so much to discover the future as to find out whether the gods approved of what they were doing on that day. Auspices could be specially sought or randomly encountered. Technically, *auspicium* meant 'bird-watching' (*avis, specio*) and birds were observed for their number, position, direction, cries and feeding. But one could also take auspices from the sky (thunder, lightning), from sacred chickens (feeding habits), from rustling leaves or reflections in a bowl of water, and so on. The state of a bull's entrails was also telling. These days hygienic vacuum-packed entrails are widely available in supermarkets across the country. Check they contain a liver and examine it for smoothness, glossiness and regular shape: if not, abandon your plans or buy another pack and try again. But taking the auspices through watching the flight of birds was perhaps the most authoritative and cheapest technique.

Orientation is vital. To take a bird augury, pitch a tent at dawn on a high hill, face south (Greeks faced north), hold a knotless stick in your right hand, pray to the gods, and identify landmarks to help section off the sky into the four quarters north, south, east and west. Transfer the stick to your left hand, and wait. Birds flying left to right are propitious, right to left unpropitious. Ravens, crows, owls and hens give

Vacuum-packed entrails

their augury by noise; eagles (the bird of Zeus), vultures, and lammergeyers by flight (very satisfactory if they come in twelves); woodpeckers and lapwings by both.

Getting the bird

Odd or threatening animal behaviour was also significant. When the Queen was hit by a kamikaze grouse on her estate in Balmoral, she dismissed the incident as trivial (the grouse it was that died). The ancients would not have been quite so confident. Since birds, having their habitat in the air, were nearer the gods than humans, it was obvious they could act as intermediaries of the divine will. So, for example, it was a bird omen that marked out Tarquinius Priscus as the next king of Rome in the seventh century BC. He was entering Rome for the first time when an eagle, gently descending, plucked his cap off, rose up squawking, swooped down again, replaced the cap, and flew off. His wife Tanaquil saw this as a mark of divine approval – Jupiter, as it were, 'crowning' him. She was right. He did indeed become the next king.

Since the eagle was the king of birds and the most trustworthy conveyor of the divine will, Her Majesty might take it as a bad sign that she was attacked by a mere grouse. But humble birds played their part too (besides, she might not have got off so lightly had an eagle careered into her). Roman armies carried chickens on campaign, for example, and before engaging with the enemy, fed them. If they ate so hungrily that the food dropped from their mouths, it was a good sign. On one famous occasion before a sea-battle, when the chickens refused to eat, the furious admiral hurled them into sea, crying 'Then let them drink!' He lost. So when the Queen was hit by that errant grouse, someone should have noted the direction it came from, angle of descent and any squawks it was making. Then someone from Lambeth Palace could have interpreted it for her.

Star laws

Heavenly signs, like showers of comets or Hale-Bopp, were particularly popular. The Latin epic poet Lucan (AD 39-65) is very sound on the metaphysical theory behind them. At the start of Book II of his epic *The Civil War* (fought between Julius Caesar and Pompey, 49-45 BC), Lucan describes how the start of the war was foreshadowed by signs and portents springing up all over the place. But Lucan then pauses in his narrative to ask why the Creator thought it necessary to send such signs in the first place. After all, their only function seems to be to make humans worry themselves to death trying to work out what on earth they might portend.

One possibility, Lucan suggests, is that the portents show that the world is being guided by a master hand towards a predetermined end (this is in tune with the Stoic philosophy of Providence or Fate, developed by the Greek Zeno in the fourth century BC). The Creator, 'binding himself by his all-controlling law', has constructed the universe in such a way that prescribed age inevitably follows prescribed age, and comets indicate the next development. On the other hand, Lucan goes on, it could be the case that nothing is ordained, but 'Chance wanders at random, bringing change after change, and accident is master of mortal affairs'. In that case, the portents indicate something is going to happen, but even the Creator does not know precisely what.

In either case, Lucan concludes, there is nothing anyone can do about it. The Creator may or may not have a plan in mind, but who can know? So there is really no point in getting into a flap about it. It is advice Julius Caesar sensibly took on the Ides of March 44 BC, as, surrounded by signs and portents, he went serenely and unflappably to his death.

God luck

Devastating natural disasters like earthquakes are 'senseless' or 'inexplicable' to us. Not, however, to the ancients.

While we think of Poseidon as god of the sea, for example, he was in fact god of the raw, violent, elemental forces of nature, and so of storms at sea, bulls, horses and especially earthquakes. In Homer, the earliest Greek literature we have (*c.* 720 BC), his almost universal title is 'earth-shaker', though he is usually active by sea (e.g. hounding Odysseus in the *Odyssey*). So it was to Poseidon that Greeks prayed during earthquakes, singing songs of praise and invoking him as 'god of security' in an attempt to appease him.

Wherever powerful or inexplicable forces were at work in the Greek world, there, as in many cultures, were the gods, with their complex range of titles (Zeus is once hailed as god of hoopoes), poetic representations (in e.g. Homer), mythologies, icon-images, worshippers, manifestations and most of all functions. Sexual activity, for example, was the domain of Aphrodite: to make love was to worship and acknowledge her. She manifested herself in e.g. flocks of sparrows, sparrow flesh being thought of as aphrodisiac. Dionysus was god of transformation, and so of alcohol and the theatre (where actors transformed themselves from one person into another). Hermes' name means 'marker-stone'. This most elusive god may best be seen as a god of boundaries and those who cross them: so of thieves, trickery, messengers, and the dead.

The fifth-century BC Greek enlightenment tried to explain the world without recourse to such gods. Thus the historian Herodotus agrees that a valley in Thessaly looks like Poseidon's work to those who fancy that sort of explanation, but concludes 'it certainly looked to me as if it was caused by an earthquake' (see p. 37). But enlightenment and superstition existed side by side throughout the ancient world, as they do in the modern. There was even a god of chance, Greek *Tukhê*, Roman *Fortuna*. She should be the sign of Camelot, the national lottery.

Fortuna was usually depicted with a cornucopia (a horn of plenty bursting with good things), a rudder, with which she steered the course of men's lives, and, to show her variability, wings or a wheel – sometimes even, perhaps anticipating the lottery, a ball. She was frequently shown blind. Most cities put up a statue to her crowned with towers to symbolise her role as guardian of the city and its prosperity.

Fortuna became increasingly important in the Roman world, and Trajan (emperor AD 98-117) put up a temple to her as the all-pervading power of the universe. When the Roman Empire officially adopted Christianity under Constantine in the fourth century AD, *Fortuna* was one of the few deities not to be displaced. She was slowly assimilated into a Christian framework and became god of Providence, symbol of the transitory nature of human success.

Time, surely, for her revival as *Fortuna Camelotensis*. But if we do not wish to adopt a Latin deity of luck, there is a perfectly good home-grown one, of British-Celtic origin. She is Ro-smerta ('Great Provider'), often shown with a bulging purse, and a statue of her in Corbridge features what looks suspiciously like a bran-tub. Still, an inscribed Roman gaming board should have the last word. 'Reject wealth: insane greed flips minds' it all too prophetically warns.

Going with the flow

There was nothing that could not be given a divine form in the ancient world and ascribed with powers that needed acknowledgement, even (for example) rivers. Ancient Greeks would have been appalled at the

Greek government's scheme to divert water from its greatest river, the Acheloos, into the plain of Thessaly, in order to encourage agriculture. Given that turbulent river's mythology, it would be difficult to think of a less advisable project.

Acheloos is the name of both the river and its god, and being the oldest river god of all he was the most demanding of respect. Universally invoked in prayers and sacrifices, famed for his sweet waters, he had a powerful temper, and when four local nymphs failed to include him in their rituals, he burst his banks and swept the women out to sea, where they turned into islands (the Echinades, on the west coast of Greece, opposite Ithaca). The force of the river was indeed legendary. When the hero Theseus was trying to cross it in a rainstorm, Acheloos counselled against it: 'My waters carry off tree-trunks, boulders, sheep-pens, herds, horses and humans', he tells the hero. Theseus wisely took his advice.

It took the only Greek man to become a god, Heracles, to restrain it. When Acheloos fell in love with a nymph Deianeira, he was miffed to find she had chosen Heracles instead. So he challenged Heracles to a wrestling match for her hand, but, despite his ability to adopt any shape he wanted, lost. Heracles promptly built embankments round the river to pen it back, both punishing the god and returning vast tracts of land to cultivation. And the Greek government is now proposing to undo the work of Heracles himself. Madness.

Divine man

Heracles was the main exception to the rule that men in the ancient world did not become gods. Nevertheless, men could still become heroised and exert malign influence from beyond the grave, unless placated (see p. 32). Take, for example, Theogenes (fifth century BC), a lesson to all jealously squabbling athletes. One of the all-time greats of the ancient games, he came from the island of Thasos. He was a boxer and all-in wrestler, remained unbeaten at boxing for twenty-two years, and was credited with 1,400 victories in all (including, amazingly, a long-distance race at the games in Argos). In recognition of his prowess, a statue of him was erected on Thasos.

After his death, however, an envious rival expressed his real feelings by flogging the statue under cover of night. The statue was having none of this, fell on the man and killed him. The man's relatives promptly took the statue to court on a murder charge. It was found guilty, taken out to sea and dumped. At once Thasos was hit by famine. The

Thasians duly consulted the oracle at Delphi and were told they had forgotten Theogenes. Not long afterwards, some fishermen quite by chance snagged their nets on the statue, so it was restored and the famine ended. The statue developed healing powers (such heroes had enough vitality even in death to spare for lesser mortals), and eight hundred years later sacrifices were still being made to it. The statue base can be seen today, fitted with metal rings: the Thasians were clearly determined not to lose it again, and chained it down.

CRACKDOWNS

In contrast to events in Ireland, religion caused unrest in the classical world only sporadically, to a limited extent with the Jews, more so with the arrival of Christianity.

Greeks and Romans did not invest their gods with unique moral, intellectual, or social authority. The gods did not pre-exist this world nor make it nor exist outside it. They emerged from it as a result of heavenly conflict. The oldest existing elements of the world included Earth (Gaia) and Sky (Ouranos = Uranus), whose copulation started filling the world with things. Ouranos was overthrown by a child of his Cronus, and Cronus in turn by Zeus. Family conflict and competition were, in true Greek fashion, built into the heavenly system (see p. 139). Between them they spawned all the other gods and powers that the ancients acknowledged, everything from Night and Death to Apollo and Artemis. Cultures get the gods they need.

The result was that Greeks and Romans were not selective about the gods they worshipped. They freely took over gods from other religions and adapted them to suit their purposes. Romans expected the peoples they conquered to take over Roman gods too. After all, the Romans had won: whose gods were the better bet?

Romans stamped on religion only when it seemed to challenge state authority. In 186 BC the cult of Bacchus flared up throughout Italy. Because of its nocturnal rites, secret meetings and incitement to debauchery, the Senate acted. Imprisonment and executions followed on a large scale, and Bacchic shrines were destroyed. But the cult was not banished: followers could still worship, with permission, in groups of five, and without a priesthood. Had Romans controlled Ireland today, they would have destroyed Irish arms' suppliers (Libya? Boston, USA?), and executed all suspect terrorists. But before the seductive process of Romanisation – *dolce vita* for the local élites, and grand new cities and hot baths for all – the churches and their leaders and suspect pubs and clubs would have been wiped out too, and future Christian cult kept small and closely monitored.

Unsafe sects

We tend to associate pagan religion with throwing people to the lions. This is not quite fair. Romans were used to religious lunatics, and, within limits, suffered them, since most of them as individuals were harmless enough. A good example of such an individualist is Peregrinus, a fame-seeking charlatan whose story is told by the Greek satirist Lucian (AD 115-180). Exiled for killing his father, Peregrinus turned 'Christian' and soon became a prophet and church-leader, interpreting their scriptures, inventing others, and revered as a god 'next to that man who was crucified in Palestine and started it all' (Lucian here comments on the ease with which the weak-minded are duped). Eventually he was thrown into prison, which gratified his desire for fame even more, since strenuous efforts were made to defend, help and rescue him. Money poured in to his coffers.

Annoyingly released without even a flogging, he decided he had milked Christians for all they were worth and now sought fame as a Cynic philosopher. He travelled the world denouncing wealth and abusing everyone, but people soon wearied of this old hat. In a final bid for glory, he announced he would commit suicide on a blazing pyre before the milling thousands at the Olympic Games 'to teach them to despise death'. This was too good to miss. The crowds rolled up (including Lucian), most of them urging him to jump. After several delays, he did so, leaving Lucian to reflect on the grip that the desire for fame had on mankind. There are many modern parallels.

The Romans wearily endured harmless individuals like Peregrinus. But it is significant that they took action against him when he associated himself with a sect (the Christians). Individuals were one thing, sects could be another, especially when they were of the murderous kind that we sometimes encounter today (one remembers David Koresh and the Waco affair in the USA).

There was no general mandate from the emperor to suppress sects. Like good pagans, Romans acknowledged numerous gods and tolerated all kinds of cult practices. But the first duty of governors was to keep their provinces peaceful, and large gatherings of people (even in markets) aroused suspicions of conspiracy. It was a particular problem in Judaea, where messiahs were ten a penny.

In the absence of an imperial policy, it was up to the individual governors to act as they saw fit. Some chose to persecute Christians, others not. Pliny the younger, governor of Bithynia AD 110-112 (modern north-western Turkey), had been receiving anonymous pamphlets naming troublesome Christians. In the absence of legal precedents, Pliny saw this as a policing issue, arrested the Christians, and ordered them to invoke pagan gods, make offerings to the emperor's statue and revile the name of Christ. When they obstinately refused what to the pagan Pliny was an entirely reasonable request, he saw it as a direct threat to Roman rule, and executed them. But the issue clearly worried him, and he wrote to Trajan (emperor AD 98-117) for help: in particular, should he punish them for *having been* Christians?

Trajan approved, adding three important riders. Christians must not be hunted down; if they repent they must be forgiven *whatever* their past conduct; and anonymous pamphlets must play no part in the proceedings. In other words, no witch hunts: the full rigour of the law must be applied. But those who put themselves *outside* the law were shown no mercy, whatever their excuses (Romans would have treated Koresh exactly as the Americans did). Roman governors found the desire for martyrdom, however, hard to handle.

Martyrs were essentially a Jewish invention of the second century BC, when those who died in the Maccabean revolt were promised instant access to the throne of God. Although Church authorities did not encourage martyrdom, it was coveted by many Christians because of the special place it guaranteed the martyr in heaven. A virgin's rewards in heaven were sixty times greater than an ordinary Christian's, a martyr's a hundred times greater. The Romans found the whole thing baffling – another example of Christian obstinacy. Many governors strenuously discouraged it.

'But wasn't St Paul [in whose *Letters* such faith was placed] just an ordinary sort of bloke who spoke Aramaic?' argued one governor to a Christian with a death-wish. 'Think it over for a few days,' ventured the governor who tried the martyr Colluthus (fourth century AD). 'Look, the weather is just lovely', he went on: 'you won't get much pleasure if you kill yourself, you know. Just listen to me, and you can save yourself.' 'My death will be more pleasant than any life you can give,' replied Colluthus, grimly. When Christians approached the governor of Asia in AD 185 demanding martyrdom, he said they could use ropes and cliffs themselves.

Christians, however, did not impose martyrdom on others, unlike so many modern 'religious' fanatics. Nor did they invite others to become martyrs while standing back themselves (Saddam Hussein promises his troops instant paradise if they die in battle, though he does not seem keen on the concept himself). Martyrdom ended by the fifth century AD, after the Roman Empire became officially Christianised.

GUILTY PARTIES

A bishop labelled as 'wicked' the hymn 'All things bright and beautiful', because it claimed that God 'ordered the estate' of the rich and the poor man. In the bishop's view, this 'lays all the blame for social problems at God's door'.

If by 'social problems' he meant poverty, the ancient Greeks were probably more in line with the bishop's thinking than the Bible. Greeks took the view that poverty tempted men to crime or other shameful behaviour. The Bible, by contrast, insisted that the poor were more likely to be happy than the wealthy, since the poor were dependent on God, while the wealthy were in danger of rating their riches above God. Greeks too thought the rich had a 'social problem', but for a different reason – wealth made them arrogant, greedy and soft.

But the classic theological question remains: what is God responsible *for*? All ancients were interested in the issue because it bore on the question of personal responsibility, but they were no more capable of solving it than we are. As the Greek thinker Protagoras (fifth century BC) dryly pointed out, reliable evidence about the gods is hard to come by.

The formulation of the epic poet Homer, however, is worth considering. In his *Iliad* and *Odyssey*, it is often impossible to distinguish between divine and human responsibility. Thus, in the *Odyssey*, the bard Phemius says 'I am self-taught and the god put in me all sorts of song-paths'. In other words, both men and gods are one hundred percent responsible for everything, all the time. Later Greek tragedians put this notion at the very centre of their tragedies. At first sight it looks illogical: but can anyone do any better?

But that did not stop Greeks worrying at the problem. The philosopher Plato (c. 429-347 BC) was most taxed by it, and his view of human responsibility emerges at the end of his *Republic* (c. 375 BC). Here he recounts what a soldier called Er, miraculously returned from the dead, said about the afterlife. It transpires that the souls' free choice of their *next* life is the key issue. Take a bow, Glenn Hoddle.

First, lots are randomly scattered among the souls to determine the order in which they select their next existence. Then the future lives (human and animal) are placed in front of them. There being more lives than souls, even the last to choose has a good pick: 'the first to choose should take care' says Hades' intermediary, 'and the last need not despair'.

At this point, Plato interjects: 'This is clearly an absolutely critical moment for a person – which is why during this life we must do everything to find someone who can tell us how to distinguish good lives from bad'. Er then goes on to describe how the first soul unhesitatingly chose the most powerful tyranny he could – not noticing it contained the fate of eating his own children and other terrible crimes. Orpheus chose to become a swan, Agamemnon an eagle, Ajax a lion, and Odysseus, tired of hardship, a humble private citizen.

They make their choices, however, with these words of Lady Lachesis, daughter of Necessity, ringing in their ears: 'Goodness makes it own rules. Each of you will be good to the extent that you value it. Responsibility lies with the chooser, not with the god.' So there.

TIME CHART

Notes

1. A Greek, i.e. a Greek speaker, could live almost anywhere in the Mediterranean, since there had been migrations and colonisation east and west from the Greek mainland from the tenth century BC onwards. Athens, just one of many self-governing city-states like Sparta, Thebes, Corinth and so on that made up ancient Greece, comes to the fore in the fifth century BC, but the Greek intellectual achievement had its foundations laid by Greek philosophers and writers inhabiting the Aegean islands and west coast of modern Turkey, especially from c. 700 BC onwards. So by 'Greek' we do not necessarily mean 'Athenian Greek'. Homer came from the coast of Turkey or an offshore island, Herodotus came from Bodrum (Turkey), Pythagoras from the island of Samos (and moved to South Italy), Hippocrates from the island of Cos, and so on.

2. Greek culture does not come to a halt when Macedon invades in the fourth century BC nor when Greece becomes a Roman province in 148 BC. These periods are marked primarily by political changes. Greek culture continues to be enormously productive and influential, and much admired by the Romans (who are ultimately responsible for its transmission to us).

3. This Time Chart covers only the main events and people dealt with in this book.

Greeks (BC)	Romans (BC)
1600-1100 *Mycenaean 'palace' culture* Bronze age. Linear B writing. 1220 Troy sacked – Homer's Troy?	
1100-950 **Period of transition** Many Mycenaean palaces sacked. Iron age. Migrations of Greeks from mainland to Aegean islands and west coast of Asia Minor (Turkey).	1000: continuous occupation of the centre of Rome.

Greeks (BC)	Romans (BC)
950-700 **Emergence of city-states** Greece slowly emerges as a collection of autonomous, self-controlled 'city-states', like Athens, Sparta, Corinth, etc. First Greek colonies founded in Bay of Naples (775) and Sicily (735). Olympic Games founded (776). *c.* 750-700 – Greeks invent first alphabet (consonants and vowels). *c.* 720-700 Homer's *Iliad* and *Odyssey*.	**753-509** **Rome under kings** Traditional date for foundation of Rome. Ruled by kings of Etruria.
700-500 **City-states controlled by single rulers (tyrants)** 594 Solon of Athens establishes new law-codes and political reforms. Earliest philosophers active in Asia Minor (Thales, Anaximander). 585 Thales predicts an eclipse. *c.* 550 Pythagoras born. *c.* 560-527 Pisistratus tyrant of Athens. 535 Polycrates tyrant of Samos. Persian menace gathers strength. 507 Cleisthenes invents democracy in Athens.	**509-31** **Roman republic** Etruscan kings expelled (after rape of Lucretia). Start of the republic and Senate control. Rome begins to take over Italy south of the Po by conquest, colonisation and alliance.
500-399 **'Classical' Athens and its empire** 490-479 Persian Wars: Persians defeated under Darius at Marathon 490; return under Xerxes in 481, defeated at Salamis 480 and Plataea 479. Athenian maritime empire develops, against Spartan land empire. 462 Pericles (*c.* 495-429) radicalises democracy. Age of Aeschylus (*c.* 525-456), Protagoras (*c.* 490-420), Hippocrates (?), Herodotus (*c.* 490-425),	

Greeks (BC)	Romans (BC)
Sophocles (*c.* 495-406), Aristophanes (*c.* 450-386), Euripides (*c.* 480-406), Thucydides (*c.* 460-400), Socrates (469-399), Pheidias (active *c.* 465-425). 432 Parthenon complete. 431-404 Athens vs. Sparta (Peloponnesian War). 431 great plague of Athens. 429 Pericles killed by plague. 404 Athens defeated by Sparta. 399 Socrates executed.	
399-323 **Demise of the city-state** Age of Plato (429-347) and Aristotle (384-322). Xenophon *c.* 430-350. 350s: Macedon to the north under King Philip II moves against the Greek states, resisted by Demosthenes (384-322). 338 Greek states capitulate. 336 Philip assassinated; his son Alexander (the Great) takes over. 334-323 Alexander takes revenge on Persia for Persian wars; marches as far as Karachi; dies in Babylon 323.	
323-31 **Hellenistic age: Greek monarchies in east** Men left in charge of areas conquered by Alexander make themselves kings, e.g. Ptolemy becomes (Greek) king of Egypt. Alexandria in Egypt rivals Athens as intellectual centre of Mediterranean under Ptolemies. Comic poet Menander 342-292. Zeno (335-263) founds Stoicism. Epicurus (341-270) founds Epicureanism.	**295:** Rome master of Italy. **264-202 Beginnings of empire** Rome defeats Carthage (North Africa) in two Punic Wars. Sicily and Spain become the first two Roman provinces. Comic poet Plautus *c.* 250-184.

Rome takes over the Mediterranean (BC)

148-146: Greece and north Africa becomes Roman provinces. Roman contact with Greek culture intensifies. Greek thinkers welcomed at Rome. Greek historian Polybius *c.* 200-118.

129: Asia bequeathed to Rome and turned into a province. Rest of what we call Turkey provincialised by 74, Syria by 63.

130-31: Republican system breaks down as powerful dynasts like Marius (157-86), Pompey (106-48), Crassus (d. 53) and Caesar (100-44) use wealth and military influence to seize control from the Senate. Cicero (106-43) active as statesman, lawyer and philosopher. **51:** Gaul becomes a province, after Caesar's conquests. **44:** Caesar assassinated: his adopted son and heir Octavian defeats Antony and Cleopatra and in 31 becomes sole ruler of Rome, and its first emperor, taking the name Augustus in 27. End of the republic.

Lucretius (*c.* 100-55), Catullus (*c.* 84-54), Horace (65-8), Virgil (70-19) and the architect Vitruvius all active.

THE ROMAN EMPIRE (BC–AD)

31-AD 14:	Augustus emperor.
	30: Egypt becomes a province.
	AD 6: Judaea becomes a province. Birth of Jesus.
	8: Ovid (43 BC–AD 17) banished.
14-37:	Tiberius emperor.
37-41:	Gaius Caligula emperor.
41-54:	Claudius emperor.
	47: Britain provincialised.
	49: younger Seneca (1-65) made tutor to Nero.
54-68:	Nero emperor (end of Julio-Claudian dynasty).
	61: Iceni in England revolt under Boudicca.
	64: great fire of Rome.
	65: younger Seneca commits suicide.
	64-68: Nero's Golden House built.
69:	Galba, Otho, Vitellius emperors (with Vespasian, 'year of the four emperors').
69-79:	Vespasian emperor.
79-81:	Titus emperor.
	79: eruption of Vesuvius. Pliny the elder (b. 23) killed investigating it.
	80: Colosseum opened.

81-96:   Domitian emperor (end of Flavian dynasty).
96-98:   Nerva emperor.
98-117:   Trajan emperor.
          Satirist Martial (b. *c.* 40) d. *c.* 104.
          100-112: Pliny the younger (61-112) governor of Bithynia
          (N. Turkey).
117-138: Hadrian emperor.
          Death of the essayist Plutarch (*c.* 46-120) and the historians
          Tacitus (*c.* 56-120) and Suetonius (*c.* 70-130).

In 392, the empire was partitioned between west and east. The last
emperor of the west was Romulus Augustus (Augustulus) 475-6. The
idea of a western Roman empire, however, continued with the collu-
sion of the Church and the Franks (Germans, now the dominant power
in Europe). In 800 Charlemagne was crowned emperor by Pope Leo II,
and from 1254 this entity was known as 'the Holy Roman Empire'. It
lasted till 1806, when King Francis II abdicated and became Franz II,
emperor of Austria.

The Roman empire in the east, based at Byzantium (re-named
Constantinople after the first Christian emperor Constantine 306-337),
lasted till May 29 1453 when the city was over-run by Ottoman Turks
under Mehmet II, and at once re-named Istanbul.

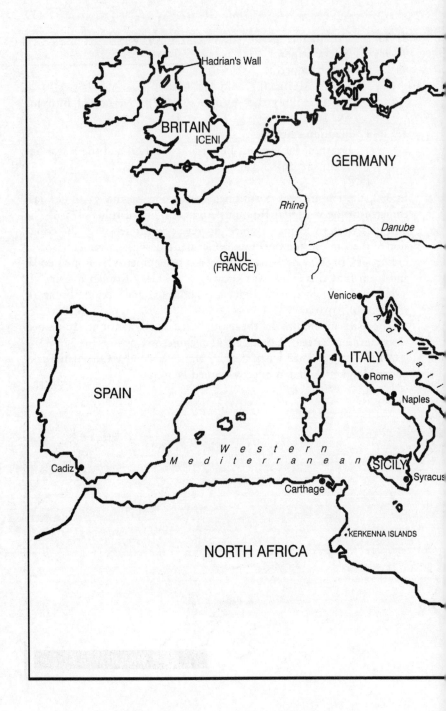

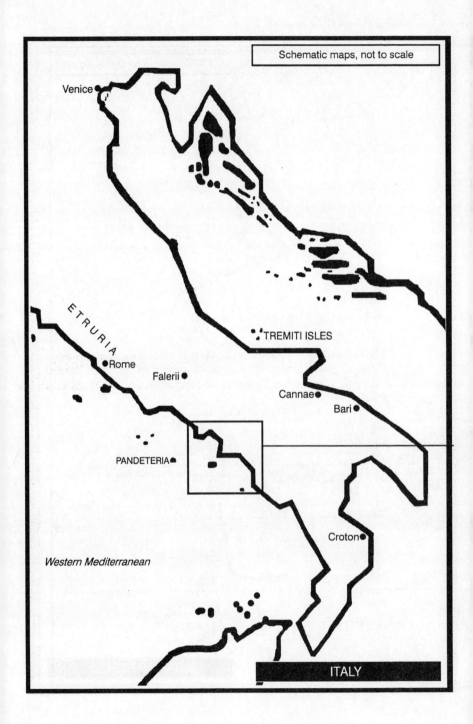

Schematic maps, not to scale

Venice

ETRURIA

Rome

Falerii

TREMITI ISLES

Cannae

Bari

PANDETERIA

Croton

Western Mediterranean

ITALY

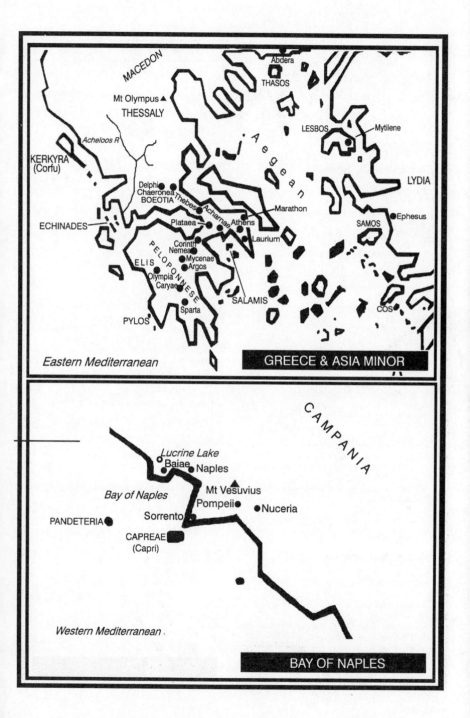

MACEDON

Abdera

THASOS

Mt Olympus ▲

THESSALY

Acheloos R

Aegean

LESBOS

Mytilene

KERKYRA
(Corfu)

LYDIA

Delphi
Chaeronea
BOEOTIA Thebes Acharnae
Marathon

Ephesus

ECHINADES

Plataea
Athens

SAMOS

Corinth
Nemea
PELOPONNESE
Laurium

ELIS
Mycenae
Argos

Olympia
Caryae
SALAMIS

COS

Sparta
PYLOS

Eastern Mediterranean

GREECE & ASIA MINOR

CAMPANIA

Lucrine Lake
Baiae
Naples

Mt Vesuvius

Bay of Naples
Pompeii
Nuceria

Sorrento

PANDETERIA

CAPREAE
(Capri)

Western Mediterranean

BAY OF NAPLES

Index

Many of the dates are approximate